The Haṭha Yoga Pradīpikā

More people are beginning to understand the efficacy and importance of going back to traditional medicine and practices like Yoga. *Hatha Yoga Pradīpikā* is a classic Sanskrit manual on Hatha Yoga, written by Swami Swatmarama in the fifteenth century. Considered to be one of the oldest surviving texts on the Hatha Yoga, it was written by Swami Swatamarama's own yogic experiences. It runs in the line of the Hindu yoga and is dedicated to Lord Adinath, a name for Lord §iva, who is alleged to have imparted the secret of Hatha Yoga to his divine consort Parvati. Explaining *asanas, pranayamas, chakras, kundalini, bandhas, kriyas, shakti, nadis* and *mudras* among other topics. This modern English translation is invaluable because it retains the original Sanskrit text.

The Haṭha Yoga Pradīpikā

Translated into English by

PANCHAM SINH

DEV PUBLISHERS & DISTRIBUTORS
New Delhi

Published by:
DEV PUBLISHERS & DISTRIBUTORS
2nd Floor, Prakash Deep,
22, Delhi Medical Association Road,
Darya Ganj,
New Delhi-110002
Phone : 011-4357 2647, 98102 36140
e-mail: devbooks@hotmail.com
website: www.devbooks.co.in

ISBN: 978-93-81406-19-9
This edition 2013

Printed in India

Contents

Introduction

There exists at present a good deal of miscon-ception with regard to the practices of the Haṭha Yoga. People easily believe in the stories told by those who themselves heard them second hand, and no attempt is made to find out the truth by a direct reference to any good treatise. It is generally believed that the six practices, (षट्कर्म) in Haṭha Yoga are compulsory on the student and that besides being dirty, they are fraught with danger to the practiser. This is not true, for these practices are necessary only in the existence of impurities in the Nāḍīs, and not otherwise.

There is the same amount of misunderstanding with regard to the Prāṇāyāma. People put their faith implicitly in the stories told them about the dangers attending the practice, without ever taking the trouble of ascertaining the fact themselves. We have been inspiring and expiring air from our birth, and will continue to do so till death; and this is done without the help of any teacher. Prāṇāyāma is nothing but a properly regulated form of the otherwise irregular and hurried flow of air, without using much force or undue restraint; and if this is accomplished by patiently keeping the flow slow and steady, there can be no danger. It is the impatience for the Siddhis which cause undue pressure on the organs and thereby causes pains in the ears, the eyes, the chest, etc. If the three bandhas (**बन्ध**) be carefully performed while practising the Prāṇāyāma, there is no possibility of any danger.

There are two classes of students of Yoga: (1) those who study it theoretically; (2) those who combine the theory with practice.

Yoga is of very little use, if studied theoretically. It was never meant for such a study. In its practical form, however, the path of the student is beset with difficulties. The books on Yoga give instructions so far as it is possible to express the methods in words, but all persons, not being careful enough to follow these instructions to the very letter, fail in their object. Such persons require a teacher versed in the practice of Yoga. It is easy to find a teacher who will explain the language of the books, but this is far from being satisfactory. For instance, a Paṇḍit without any knowledge of the science of Materia Medica will explain **कंटकारि** as **कंटकस्यारिः कंटकारिः** or an enemy of thorns, *i.e.*, shoes, while it is in reality the name of a medicinal plant.

The importance of a practical Yogī as a guide to a student of Yoga cannot be overestimated; and without such a teacher it is next to impossible for him to achieve anything. The methods followed by the founders of the system and followed ever afterwards by their followers, have been wisely and advisedly kept secret; and this is not without a deep meaning. Looking to the gravity of the subject and the practices which have a very dose relation with the vital organs of the human body, it is of paramount importance that the instructions should be received by students of ordinary capacity, through a practical teacher only, in order to avoid any possibility of mistake in practice. Speaking broadly, all men are not equally fitted to receive the instructions on equal terms. Man inherits on birth his mental and physical capitals, according to his actions in past births, and has to increase them by manipulation, but there are, even among such, different grades. Hence, one cannot become a Yogī in one incarnation, as says Śrī Kṛṣṇa **बहूनांजन्मनामन्ते मामप्रपद्यतिभारत।** and again **मनुष्याणां सहस्रेषु कश्चिद्यतति सिद्धये। यततामपिसिद्धरनां कश्चिन्माम्वेत्ति तत्त्वतः॥ गीता॥**

There are men who, impelled by the force of their actions of previous births, go headlong and accomplish their liberation in a single attempt; but others have to earn it in their successive births. If the student belongs to one of such souls and being earnest, desires from his heart to get rid of the pains of birth and death, he will find the means too. It is well-known that a true Yogī is above temptations and so to think that he keeps his knowledge secret for selling it to the highest bidder is simply absurd. Yoga is meant for the good of all creatures, and a true Yogī is always desirous of benefitting as many men as possible. But he is not to throw away this precious treasure indiscriminately. He carefully chooses its recipients, and when be finds a true and earnest student, who will not trifle with this knowledge, he never hesitates in placing his valuable treasure at the disposal of the man. What is essential in him is that he should have a real thirst for such knowledge—a thirst which will make him restless till satisfied; the thirst that will make him blind to the world and its enjoyments. He should be, in short, fired with **मुमुक्षुत्व** or desire for emancipation. To such a one, there is nothing dearer than the accomplishment of this object. A true lover will risk his very life to gain union with his beloved like Tulasīdās. A true lover will see everywhere, in every direction, in every tree and leaf, in every blade of grass his own beloved. The whole of the world, with all its beauties, is a dreary waste in his eyes, without his beloved. And he will court death, fall into the mouth of a gaping grave, for the sake of his beloved. The student whose heart burns with such intense desire for union with Paramātmā, is sure to find a teacher, and through him he will surely find Him. It is a tried experience that Paramātmā will try to meet you half way, with the degree of intensity with which you will go to meet Him. Even He Himself will become your guide, direct you on to the road to success, or put you on the track to find a teacher, or lead him to you.

Well has it been said **जिन ढूंढा तिन पाइयाँ गहरे पानी पैठि। मैं बावरि ढूंढन चली रही किनारे बैठि।।** It is the half-hearted who fail. They hold their worldly pleasures dearer to their hearts than their God, and therefore He in His turn does not consider them worthy of His favours, Says the Upaniṣad :—

नायमात्मा प्रवचनेन लभ्यो न मेधया न बहुना श्रुतेन। यमेवैष वृणुते तेनलभ्यस्तस्यैष आत्मा विवृणुते तनुस्वाम्।।

The ātmā will choose you its abode only if it considers you worthy of such a favour, and not otherwise. It is therefore necessary that one should first make oneself worthy of His acceptance, Having prepared the temple (your heart) well fitted for His installation there, having cleared it of all the impurities which stink and make the place unsuitable for the highest personage to live in, and having decorated it beautifully with objects as befit that Lord of the creation, you need not wait long for Him to adorn this temple of yours which you have taken pains to make it worthy of Him. If you have done all this, He will shine in you in all His glory. In your difficult moments, when you are embarrassed, sit in a contemplative mood, and approach your Parama Guru submissively and refer your difficulties to Him, you are sure to get the proper advice from Him. He is the Guru of the ancients, for He is not limited by Time. He instructed the ancients in bygone times, like a Guru, and if you have been unable to find a teacher in the human form, enter your inner temple and consult this Great Guru who accompanies you everywhere, and ask Him to show you the way. He knows best what is best for you. Unlike mortal beings, He is beyond the past and the future, will either send one of His agents to guide you or lead you to one and put you on the right track. He is always anxious to teach the earnest seekers, and waits for you to offer Him an opportunity to do so. But if you have not done your duty and prepared yourself worthy of entering His door, and try to gain access to His presence, laden with you unclean burden, stinking with Kāma, Krodha, Lobha, and Moha, be sure He will keep you off from Him.

The Āsanas are a means of gaining steadiness of position and help to gain success in contemplation, without any distraction of the mind. If the position be not comfortable, the slightest inconvenience will draw the mind away from the lakṣya (aim), and so no peace of mind will be possible till the posture has ceased to cause pain by regular exercise.

Of all the various methods for concentrating the mind, repetition of Praṇava or Ajapā Jāpa and contemplation on its meaning is the best. It is impossible for the mind to sit idle even for a single moment, and, therefore, in order to keep it well occupied and to keep other antagonistic thoughts from entering it, repetition of Praṇava should be practised. It should be repeated till Yoga Nidrā is induced which, when experienced, should be encouraged by slackening all the muscles of the body. This will fill the mind with sacred and divine thoughts and will bring about its one-pointedness, without much effort.

Anāhata Nāda is awakened by the exercise of Prāṇāyāma. A couple of weeks' practice with 80 prāṇāyāmas in the morning and the same number in the evening will cause distinct sounds to be heard; and, as the practice will go on increasing, varied sounds become audible to the practiser. By hearing these sounds attentively one gets concentration of the mind, and thence Sahaja Samādhi. When Yoga sleep is experienced, the student shonld give himself up to it and make no efforts to check it. By and by, these sounds become subtle and they bocome less and less intense, so the mind loses its waywardness and becomes calm and docile; and, on this practice becoming well-established, Samādhi becomes a voluntary act. This is, however, the highest stage and is the lot of the favoured and fortunate few only.

During contemplation one sees, not with his eyes, as he does the objects of the world, various colours, which the writers on Yoga call the colours of the five elements. Sometimes stars are seen glittering, and lightning flashes in the sky. But these are all fleeting in their nature.

At first these colours are seen in greatly agitated waves which show the unsteady condition of the mind; and as the practice increases and the mind becomes calm, these colour-waves become steady and motionless and appear as one deep ocean of light. This is the ocean in which one should dive and forget the world and become one with his Lord—which is the condition of highest bliss.

Faith in the practices of Yoga, and in one's own powers to accomplish what others have done before, is of great importance to insure speedy success. I mean "faith that will move mountains," will accomplish anything, be it howsoever difficult. There is nothing which cannot be accomplished by practice. Says Śiva in Śiva Saṁhitā.

अभ्यासाज्जायते सिद्धिरभ्यासान्मोक्षमाप्नुयात्॥
संविदंलभतेऽभ्यासा द्योगोभ्यसात्प्रवर्तते।
मुद्राणांसिद्धिरभ्यासा दभ्यासाद्वायुसाधनम्॥
कालवञ्चनमभ्यासात्तथामृत्युञ्जयोभवेत्।
वाक्सिद्धिः कामचारित्वं भवेदभ्यासयोगतः॥

अ. ३ श्लोक ९-११

Through practice success is obtained; through practice one gains liberation.

Perfect consciousness is gained through practice; Yoga is attained through practice; success in mudrās comes by practice. Through practice is gained success in prāṇāyāma. Death can be evaded of its prey through practice, and man becomes the conqueror of death by practice. And then let us gird up our loins, and with a firm resolution engage in the practice, having faith in **कर्मण्येवाधिकारस्ते मा फलेषु कदाचन,** and the success must be ours. May the Almighty Father, be pleased to shower His blessings on those who thus engage in the performance of their duties. Om Śam.

PANCHAM SINH

Ajmer
31st January, 1915

Chapter I

प्रथमोपदेशः

On Āsanas

श्रीआदिनाथाय नमोऽस्तु तस्मै येनोपदिष्टा हठयोगविद्या।
विभ्राजते प्रोन्नतराजयोगमारोढुमिच्छोरधिरोहिणीव॥ १॥

1. Salutation to Ādinātha (Śiva) who expounded the knowledge of Haṭha Yoga, which like a staircase leads the aspirant to the high pinnacled Rāja Yoga.

प्रणम्य श्रीगुरुं नाथं स्वात्मारमेण योगिना।
केवलं राजयोगाय हठविद्योपदिश्यते॥ २॥

2. Yogic Svātmārāma, after salutinig first his Guru Śrīnātha explains Haṭha Yoga for the attainment of Rāja Yoga.

भ्रांत्या बहुमतध्वांते राजयोगमजानताम्।
हठप्रदीपिकां धत्ते स्वात्मारामः कृपाकरः॥ ३॥

3. Owing to the darkness arising from the multiplicity of opinions people are unable to know the Rāja Yoga. Compassionate Svātmārāma composes the Haṭha Yoga Pradīpikā like a torch to dispel it.

हठविद्यां हि मत्स्येंद्रगोरक्षाद्या विजानते।
स्वात्मारामोऽथवा योगी जानीते तत्प्रसादतः॥ ४॥

4. Matsyendra, Gorakṣa, etc., knew Haṭha Vidyā, and by their favour Yogī Svātmārāma also leant it from them.

श्रीआदिनाथमत्स्येंद्रशाबरानंदभैरवाः।
चौरंगी मीनगोरक्षविरूपाक्षबिलेशयाः॥ ५॥

5. The following Siddhas (masters) are said to have existed in former times :—

Śrī Ādinātha (Śiva), Matayendra Nātha, Śābara, Ānanda, Bhairava, Cauraṅgī, Mīnanātha, Gorakṣa-nātha, Virupākṣa, Bileśaya.

मंथानो भैरवो योगी सिद्धर्बुद्धश्च कंथडिः।
कोरंटकः सुरानंदः सिद्धपादश्च चर्पटिः॥ ६॥

6. Manthāna, Bhairava, Siddhi Buddha, Kanthaḍi, Karaṇṭaka, Surānanda, Siddhapāda, Carpaṭi.

कानेरी पूज्यपादश्च नित्यनाथो निरंजनः।
कपाली बिंदुनाथश्च काकचंडीश्वराव्हयः॥ ७॥

7. Kānerī, Pūjyapāda, Nityanātha, Nirañjana, Kapālī, Bindunātha, Kāka Caṇḍīśvara.

अल्लामः प्रभुदेवश्च घोडाचोली च टिंटिणिः।
भानुकी नारदेवश्च खंडः कापालिकस्तथा॥ ८॥

8. Allāma, Prabhudeva, Ghoḍā, Colī, Ṭinṭiṇi, Bhānukī, Nāradeva, Khaṇḍa Kāpālika, etc.

इत्यादयो महासिद्धा हठयोगप्रभावतः।
खंडयित्वा कालदंडं ब्रह्मांडे विचरंति ते॥ ९॥

9. These Mahāsiddhas (great masters), breaking the sceptre of death, are roaming in the universe.

अशेषतापतप्तानां समाश्रयमठो हठः।
अशेषयोगयुक्तानामाधारकमठो हठः॥ १०॥

10. Like a house protecting one from the heat of the sun, Haṭha Yoga protects its practiser from the burning heat of the three Tāpas; and, similarly, it is the supporting tortoise, as it were, for those who are constantly devoted to the practice of Yoga.

हठविद्या परं गोप्या योगिना सिद्धिमिच्छता।
भवेद्वीर्यवती गुप्ता निर्वीर्या तु प्रकाशिता॥ ११॥

11. A Yogī desirous of success should keep the knowledge of Haṭha Yoga secret; for it becomes potent by concealing, and impotent by exposing.

सुराज्ये धार्मिके देशे सुभिक्षे निरुपद्रवे।
धनुः प्रमाणपर्यंतं शिलाग्निजलवर्जिते।
एकांते मठिकामध्ये स्थातव्यं हठयोगिना॥ १२॥

12. The Yogī should practise Haṭha Yoga in a small room, situated in a solitary place, being 4 cubits square, and free from stones, fire, water, disturbances of all kinds, and in a country where justice is properly administered, where good people live, and food can be obtained easily and plentifully.

अल्पद्वारमरंध्रगर्तविवरं नात्युच्चनीचायतं।
सम्यग्गोमयसांद्रलिप्तममलं निःशेषजंतूज्झितम्।
बाह्ये मंडपवेदिकूपरुचिरं प्राकारसंवेष्टितं
प्रोक्तं योगमठस्य लक्षणमिदं सिद्धैर्हठाभ्यासिभिः॥ १३॥

13. The room should have a small door, be free from holes, hollows, neither too high nor too low, well plastered with cow-dung and free from dirt, filth and insects. On its outside there should be bowers, raised platform (cabūtrā), a well, and a compound. These characteristics of a room for Haṭha Yogīs have been described by adepts in the practice of Haṭha.

एवंविधे मठे स्थित्वा सर्वचिंताविवर्जितः।
गुरूपदिष्टमार्गेण योगमेव समभ्यसेत्॥ १४॥

14. Having seated in such a room and free from all anxieties, he should practise Yoga, as instructed by his *guru*.

अत्याहारः प्रयासश्च प्रजल्पो नियमग्रहः।
जनसंगश्च लौल्यं च षडभिर्योगो विनश्यति॥ १५॥

15. Yoga is destroyed by the following six

causes :— Overeating, exertion, talkativeness, adhering to rule, *i.e.*, cold bath in the morning, eating at night, or eating fruits only, company of men, and unsteadiness.

उत्साहात्साहसाद्धैर्यात्तत्त्वज्ञानाच्च निश्चयात्।
जनसंगपरित्यागात्षड्भिर्योगः प्रसिद्ध्यति॥ १६॥

16. The following six bring speedy success :— Courage, daring, perseverance, discriminative knowledge, faith, aloofness from company.

अथ यमनियमाः

अहिंसा सत्यमस्तेयं ब्रह्मचर्यं क्षमा धृतिः।
दयार्जवं मिताहारः शौचं चैव यमा दश॥ १७॥

17. The ten rules of conduct are : ahiṁsā (non-injuring), truth, non-stealing, continence, forgiveness, endurance, compassion, meekness, sparing diet and cleanliness.

तपः संतोष आस्तिक्यं दानमीश्वरपूजनम्।
सिद्धांतवाक्यश्रवणं ह्रीमती च तपो हुतम्।
नियमा दश संप्रोक्ता योगशास्त्रविशारदैः॥ १८॥

18. The ten niyamas mentioned by those proficient in the knowledge of yoga are : Tapa, patience, belief in God, charity, adoration of God, hearing discourses on the principles of religion, shame, intellect, Tapa and Yajña.

अथ आसनम्

हठस्य प्रथमांगत्वादासनंपूर्वमुच्यते।
कुर्यात्तदासनं स्थैर्यमारोग्यं चांगलाघवम्॥ १९॥

Āsanas

19. Being the first accessory of Haṭha Yoga, āsana is described first. It should be practised for gaining steady posture, health and lightness of body.

वसिष्ठाद्यैश्च मुनिभिर्मत्स्येंद्राद्यैश्च योगिभिः।
अंगीकृतान्यासनानि कथ्यं ते कानिचिन्मया॥ २०॥

20. I am going to describe certain āsanas which have been adopted by Munis like Vasiṣṭha, etc., and Yogīs like Matsyendra, etc.

जानूर्वोरंतरे सम्यक्कृत्वा पादतले उभे।
ऋजुकायः समासीनः स्वस्तिकं तत्प्रचक्षते॥ २१॥

Svastika-āsana

21. Having kept both the hands under both the thighs, with the body straight, when one sits calmly in this posture, it is called Svastika.

सव्ये दक्षिणगुल्फं तु पृष्ठपार्श्वे नियोजयेत्।
दक्षिणेऽपि तथा सव्यं गोमुखं गोमुखाकृति॥ २२॥

Gomukha-āsana

22. Placing the right ankle on the left side and the left ankle on the right side, makes Gomukha-āsana, having the appearance of a cow.

एकं पादं तथैकस्मिन्विन्यसेदूरुणि स्थितम्।
इतरस्मिंस्तथा चोरुं वीरासनमितीरितम्॥ २३॥

Vīrāsana

23. One foot is to be placed on the thigh of the opposite side; and so also the other foot on the opposite thigh. This is called Vīrāsana.

गुदं निरुद्ध्य गुल्फाभ्यां व्युत्क्रमेण समाहितः।
कूर्मासनं भवेदेतदिति योगविदो विदुः॥ २४॥

Kūrmāsana

24. Placing the right ankle on the left side of anus, and the left ankle on the right side of it, makes what the Yogīs call Kūrma-āsana.

पद्मासनं तु संस्थाप्य जानूर्वोरंतरे करौ।
निवेश्य भूमौ संस्थाप्य कुक्कुटासनम्॥ २५॥

Kukkuṭa āsana

25. Taking the posture of Padma-āsana and carrying the hands under the thighs, when the Yogī raises himself above the ground, with his palms resting on the ground, it becomes Kukkuṭa-āsana.

कुक्कुटासनबंधस्थो दोर्भ्यां संबध्य कंधराम्।
भवेत्कूर्मवदुत्तान एतदुत्तानकूर्मकम्।। २६।।

Uttāna Kūrma-āsana

26. Having assumed Kukkuṭa-āsana, when one grasps his neck by crossing his hands behind his head, and lies in this posture with his back touching the ground, it becomes Uttāna Kūrma-āsana, from its appearance like that of a tortoise.

पादांगुष्ठौ तु पाणिभ्यां गृहीत्व श्रवणावधि।
धनुराकर्षणं कुर्याद्धनुरासमुच्यते।। २७।।

Dhanura āsana

27. Having caught the toes of the feet with both the hands and carried them to the ears by drawing the body like a bow, it becomes Dhanura āsana.

वामोरुमूलार्पितदक्षपादं जानोर्बहिर्वेष्टितवामपादम्।
प्रगृह्य तिष्ठेत्परिवर्तितांगः श्रीमत्स्यनाथोदितमासनं स्यात्।। २८।।
मत्स्येंद्रपीठं जठरप्रदीप्तिं प्रचंडरुग्मंडलखंडनास्त्रम्।
अभ्यासतः कुंडलिनीप्रबोधं चंद्रस्थिरत्वं च ददाति पुंसाम्।। २९।।

Matsya āsana

28–29. Having placed the right foot at the root of the left thigh, let the toe be grasped with the right hand passing over the back, and having placed the left foot on the right thigh at its root, let it be grasped with the left hand passing behind the back. This is the āsana, as explained by Śrī Matsyanātha. It increases appetite and is an instrument for destroying the group of the most deadly diseases. Its practice awakens the Kuṇḍalinī, stops the nectar shedding from the moon in people.

प्रसार्य पादौ भुवि दंडरूपौ दोर्भ्यां पदाग्रद्वितयं गृहीत्वा।
जानूपरि न्यस्तललाटदेशो वसेदिदं पश्चिमतानमाहुः॥ ३०॥

Paścima Tāna

30. Having stretched the feet on the ground, like a stick, and having grasped the toes of both the feet with both the hands, when one sits with his forehead resting on the thighs, it is called Paścima Tāna.

इति पश्चिमतानमासनाग्र्यं पवनं पश्चिमवाहिनं करोति।
उदयं जठरानलस्य कुर्यादुदरे कार्श्यमरोगतां च पुंसाम्॥ ३१॥

31. This Paścima Tāna carries the air from the front to the back part of the body (*i.e.*, to the suṣumnā). It kindles gastric fire, reduces obesity and cures all diseases of men.

धरामवष्टभ्य करद्वयेन तत्कूर्परस्थापितनाभिपार्श्वः॥
उच्चासनो दंडवदुत्थितः स्यान्मयूरमेतत्प्रवदंति पीठम्॥ ३२॥

Mayūra āsana

32. Place the palms of both the hands on the ground, and place the navel on both the elbows and balancing thus, the body should be stretched backward like a stick. This is called Mayūra-āsana.

हरतिसकलरोगानाशु गुल्मोदरादीनभि-
भवति च दोषानासनं श्रीमयूरम्।
बहु कदशनभुक्तं भस्म कुर्यादशेषं
जनयति जठराग्निं जारयेत्कालकूटम्॥ ३३॥

33. This āsana soon destroys all diseases, and removes abdominal disorders, and also those arising from irregularities of phlegm, bile and wind, digests unwholesome food taken in excess, increases appetite and destroys the most deadly poison.

उत्तानं शववद्भूमौ शयनं तच्छवासनम्।
शवासनं श्रांतिहरं चित्तविश्रांतिकारकम्॥ ३४॥

Śava āsana

34. Lying down on the ground, like a corpse, is called Śava-āsana. It removes fatigue and gives rest to the mind.

चतुरशीत्यासनानि शिवेन कथितानि च।
तिभ्यश्चतुष्कमादाय सारभूतं ब्रवीम्यहम्॥ ३५॥

35. Śiva taught 84 āsanas. Of these the first four being essential ones, I am going to explain them here.

सिद्धं पद्मं तथा सिंहं भद्रं चेति चतुष्टयम्।
श्रेष्ठं तत्रापि च सुखे तिष्ठेत्सिद्धासने सदा॥ ३६॥

36. These four are :—The Siddha, Padma, Siṁha and Bhadra. Even of these, the Siddha-āsana, being very comfortable, one should always practise it.

योनिस्थानकमंघ्रिनमूलघटितं कृत्वा दृढं विन्यसेत्
मेंढ्रे पादमथैकमेव हृदये कृत्वाहनु सुस्थिरम्।
स्थाणुः संयमितेंद्रियोऽचलदृशा पश्येद्भ्रुवोरंतरं
ह्येतन्मोक्षकपाटभेदजननं सिद्धासनं प्रोच्यते॥ ३७॥

The Siddhāsana

37. Press firmly the heel of the left foot against the perineum, and the right heel above the male organ. With the chin pressing on the chest, one should sit calmly, having restrained the senses, and gaze steadily the space between the eyebrows. This is called the Siddha Āsana, the opener of the door of salvation.

मतांतरे तु
मेंढ्रादुपरि विनयस्य सव्यं गुल्फं तथोपरि।
गुल्फांतरं च निक्षिप्य सिद्धासनमिदं भवेत्॥ ३८॥

38. This Siddhāsana is performed also by placing

the left heel on Meḍhra (above the male organ), and then placing the right one on it.

एतत्सिद्धासनं प्राहुरन्ये वज्रासनं विदुः।
मुक्तासनं वदंत्येके प्राहुर्गुप्तासनं परे॥ ३९॥

39. Some call this Siddhāsana, some Vajrāsana. Others call it Mukta Āsana or Gupta Āsana.

यमेष्विव मिताहारमहिंसां नियमेष्विव।
मुख्यं सर्वासनेष्वेकंसिद्धाः सिद्धासनं विदुः॥ ४०॥

40. Just as sparing food is among Yamas, and Ahiṁsā among the Niyamas, so is Siddhāsana called by adepts the chief of all the āsanas.

चतुरशीतिपीठेषु सिद्धमेव सदाभ्यसेत्॥
द्वासप्ततिसहस्राणां नाडीनां मलशोधनम्॥ ४१॥

41. Out of the 84 Āsanas Siddhāsana should always be practised, because it cleanses the impurities of 72,000 nāḍīs.

आत्मध्यायी मिताहारी यावद्द्वादशवत्सरम्।
सदा सिद्धासनाभ्यासाद्योगी निष्पत्तिमाप्नुयात्॥ ४२॥

42. By contemplating on oneself, by eating sparingly, and by practising Siddhāsana for 12 years, the Yogī obtains success.

किमन्यैर्बहुभिः पीठैः सिद्धे सिद्धासने सति।
प्राणानिले सावधाने बद्धे केवलकुंभके॥ ४३॥

43. Other postures are of no use, when success has been achieved in Siddhāsana, and Prāṇa Vāyu becomes calm and restrained by Kevala Kumbhaka.

उत्पद्यते निरायासात्स्वयमेवोन्मनी कला।
तथैकस्मिन्नेव दृढे सिद्धे सिद्धासने सति।
बंधत्रयमनायासात्स्वयमेवोपजायते॥ ४४॥

44. Success in one Siddhāsana alone becoming firmly established, one gets Unmanī at once, and the three bonds (Bandhas) are accomplished of themselves.

नासनं सिद्धसदृशं न कुंभः केवलोपमः।
न खेचरीसमा मुद्रा न नादसदृशो लयः॥ ४५॥

45. There is no Āsana like the Siddhāsana and no Kumbhaka like the Kevala. There is no mudrā like the Khecarī and no *laya* a like the Nāda (Anāhata Nāda.)

अथ पद्मासनं
वामोरूपरि दक्षिणं च चरणं संथाप्य वामं तथा
दक्षो रूपरि पश्चिमेन विधिना धृत्वा कराभ्यां दृढम्।
अंगुष्ठौ हृदये निधाय चिबुकं नासाग्रमालोकयेत्
एतद्व्याधिविनाशकारि यमिनां पद्मासनं प्रोच्यते॥ ४६॥

Padmāsana

46. Place the right foot on the left thigh, and the left foot on the right thigh, and grasp the toes with the hands crossed over the back. Press the chin against the chest and gaze on the tip of the nose. This is called the Padmāsana, the destroyer of the diseases of the Yamīs.

उत्तानौ चरणौ कृत्वा ऊरुसंस्थौ प्रयत्नतः।
ऊरुमध्ये तथोत्तानौ पाणी कृत्वा ततो दृशौ॥ ४७॥

47. Place the feet on the thighs, with the soles upwards, and place the hands on the thighs, with the palms upwards.

नासाग्रे विन्यसेद्राजदंतमूले तु जिह्वया।
उत्तंभ्य चिबुकं वक्षस्युत्थाप्य पवनं शनैः॥ ४८॥

48. Gaze on the tip of the nose, keeping the tongue pressed against the root of the teeth of the upper jaw, and the chin against the chest, and raise the air up slowly, *i.e.*, pull the apāna-vāyu gently upwards.

इदं पद्मासनं प्रोक्तं सर्वव्याधिविनाशनम्।
दुर्लभं येन केनापि धीमता लभ्यते भुवि॥ ४९॥

49. This is called the Padmāsana, the destroyer of all diseases. It is difficult of attainment by everybody, but can be learnt by intelligent people in this world.

कृत्वा संपुटितौ करौ दृढतरं बध्वा तु पद्मासनं
गाढं वक्षसि सन्निधाय चिबुकं ध्यायंश्च तच्चेतसि॥
वारं वारमपानमूर्ध्वमनिलं प्रोत्सारयन्पूरितं
न्यंचन्प्राणमुपैति बोधमतुलं शक्तिप्रभावान्नरः॥ ५०॥

50. Having kept both the hands together in the lap, performing the Padmāsana firmly, keeping the chin fixed to the chest and contemplating on Him in the mind, by drawing the apāna-vāyu up (performing Mūla Bandha) and pushing down the air after inhaling it, joining thus the prāṇa and apāna in the navel, one gets the highest intelligence by awakening the śakti (kuṇḍalinī) thus.

N.B.—When Apāna Vāyu is drawn gently up and after filling in the lungs with the air from outside, the prāṇa is forced down by and by so as to join both of them in the navel, they both enter then the Kuṇḍalinī and, reaching the Brahma randhra (the great hole), they make the mind calm. Then the mind can contemplate on the nature of the ātmana and can enjoy the highest bliss.

पद्मासने स्थितो योगी नाडीद्वारेण पूरितम्।
मारुतं धारयेद्यस्तु स मुक्तो नात्र संशयः॥ ५१॥

51. The Yogī who, sitting with Padmāsana, can control breathing, there is no doubt, is free from bondage.

अथ सिंहासनं

गुल्फौ च वृषणास्याधः सीवन्याः पार्श्वयोः क्षिपेत्।
दक्षिणे सव्यगुल्फं तु दक्षगुल्फं तु सव्यके॥ ५२॥

The Siṁhāsana

52. Press the heels on both sides of the seam of Perineum, in such a way that the left heel touches the right side and the right heel touches the left side of it.

हस्तौ तु जान्वोः संस्थाप्य स्वांगुलीः संप्रसार्य च।
व्यात्तवक्त्रो निरीक्षेत नासाग्रं सुसमाहितः॥ ५३॥

53. Place the hands on the thighs, with stretched fingers, and keeping the mouth open and the mind collected, gaze on the tip of the nose.

सिंहासनं भवेदेतत्पूजितं योगिपुंगवैः।
बंधत्रितयसंधानं कुरुते चासनोत्तमम्॥ ५४॥

54. This is Siṁhāsana, held sacred by the best of Yogīs. This excellent Āsana effects the completion of the three Bandhas (The Mūlabandha, Kaṇṭha or Jālandhara Bandha and Uḍḍīyāna Bandha).

अथ भद्रासनं

गुल्फौ च वृषणस्याधः सीवन्याः पार्श्वयोः क्षिपेत्।
सव्यगुल्फं तथा सव्ये दक्षगुल्फं तु दक्षिणे॥ ५५॥
पार्श्वपादौ च पाणिभ्यां दृढं बध्वा सुनिश्चलम्।
भद्रासनं भवेदेतत्सर्वव्याधिविनाशनम्॥ ५६॥

The Bhadrāsana

55–56. Place the heels on either side of the seam of the Perineum, keeping the left heel on the left side and the right one on the right side, hold the feet firmly joined to one another with both the hand. This Bhadrāsana is the destroyer of all the diseases.

गोरक्षासनमित्याहुरिदं वै सिद्धयोगिनः।
एवमासनबंधेषु योगींद्रो विगतश्रमः॥ ५७॥

57. The expert Yogīs call this Gorakṣa āsana. By sitting with this āsana, the Yogī gets rid of fatigue.

अभ्यसेन्नाडिकाशुद्धिं मुद्रादिपवनक्रियाम्।

आसनं कुंभकं चित्रं मुद्राख्यं करणं तथा॥ ५८॥

58. The Nāḍīs should be cleansed of their impurities by performing the mudrās, etc., (which are the practices relating to the air) Āsanas, Kumbhakas and various curious mudrās.

अथ नादानुसंधानमभ्यासानुक्रमो हठे।
ब्रह्मचारी मिताहारी त्यागी योगपरायणः।
अब्दादूर्ध्वं भवेत्सिद्धो नात्र कार्या विचारणा॥ ५९॥

59. By regular and close attention to Nāda (anāhata nāda) in Haṭha Yoga, a Brahmacārī, sparing in diet, unattached to objects of enjoyment, and devoted to Yoga, gains success, no doubt, within a year.

सुस्निग्धमधुराहारश्चतुर्थांश विवर्जितः।
भुज्यते शिवसंप्रीत्यै मिताहारः स उच्यते॥ ६०॥

60. Abstemious feeding is that in which ¾ of hunger is satisfied with food, well cooked with ghee and sweets, and eaten with the offering of it to Śiva.

कट्वम्ल तीक्ष्ण लवणोष्ण हरीतशाक
सौवीरतैलतिलसर्षप मद्य मत्स्यान्।
आजादि मांस दधि तक्र कुलत्थ कोल
पिण्याक हिंगु लशुनाद्य मपथ्य माहुः॥ ६१॥

Foods injurious to a Yogī

61. Bitter, sour, saltish, hot, green vegetables, fermented, oily, mixed with til seed, rape seed, intoxicating liquors, fish, meat, curds, chāsa pulses, plums, oil-cake, asafoetida (hīṅga), garlic, onion, etc., should not be eaten.

भोजनमहितं विद्यात्पुनरस्योष्णीकृतं रुक्षम्।
अतिलवणमम्लयुक्तं कदशनशाकोत्कटं वर्ज्यम्।
वह्निस्त्रीपथिसेवानामादौ वर्जनमाचरेत्॥ ६२॥

62. Food heated again, dry, haying too much salt,

sour, minor grains, and vegetables that cause burning sensation, should not be eaten.

Fire, women, travelling, etc., should be avoided.

तथाहि गोरक्षवचनं

वर्जयेदुर्जनप्रांतंवन्हि स्त्री पथिसेवनम्॥

प्रातःस्नानोपवासादि कायक्लेशविधिं तथा॥ ६३॥

63. As said by Gorakṣa, one should keep aloof from the society of the evil-minded, fire, women, travelling, early morning bath, fasting, and all kinds of bodily exertion.

गोधूम शालि यव षाष्टिकशोभनान्नं।

क्षीराज्यखडं नवनीत सितामधूनि।

शुंठपटोलकफलादिक पंच शाकं।

मुद्गादिदिव्यमुदकं च यमींद्रपथ्यम्॥ ६४॥

64. Wheat, rice, barley, ṣāṣṭika (a kind of rice), good corns, milk, ghee, sugar, butter, sugarcandy, honey, dried ginger, Parwal (a vegetable) the five vegetables, mooṅg, pure water, these are very beneficial to those who practise Yoga.

पुष्टं सुमधुरं स्निग्धं गव्यं धातुप्रपोषणाम्।

मनोभिलषितं योग्यं योगी भोजनमाचरेत्॥ ६५॥

65. A Yogī should eat tonics (things giving strength), well sweetened, greasy (made with ghee), milk, butter, etc., which may increase humors of the body, according to his desire.

युवा वृद्धोऽतिवृद्धो वा व्याधितो दुर्बलोऽपि वा।

अभ्यासात्सिद्धिमाप्नोति सर्वयोगेष्वतंद्रितः॥ ६६॥

66. Whether young, old or too old, sick or lean, one who discards laziness, gets success if he practises Yoga.

क्रियायुक्तस्य सिद्धिः स्यादक्रियस्य कथं भवेत्।

न शास्त्रपाठमात्रेण योगसिद्धिः प्रजायते॥ ६७॥

67. Success comes to him who is engaged in the practice. How can one get success without practice; for by merely reading books on Yoga, one can never get success.

न वेषधारणं सिद्धेः कारणं न च तत्कथा।
क्रियैव कारणं सिद्धेः सत्यमेतन्न संशयः॥ ६८॥

68. Success cannot be attained by adopting a particular dress (Veṣa). It cannot be gained by telling tales. Practice alone is the means to success. This is true, there is no doubt.

पीठानि कुंभकाश्चित्रा दिव्यानि करणानि च।
सर्वाण्यपि हठाभ्यासे राजयोगफलावधि॥ ६९॥

69. Āsanas (postures), various Kumbhakas, and other divine means, all should be practised in the practice of Haṭha Yoga, till the fruit—Rāja Yoga—is obtained.

इति हठप्रदीपिकायाम् प्रथमोपदेशः॥

End of chapter I, on the method of forming the Āsanas.

Chapter II

द्वितीयोपदेशः

On Prāṇāyāma

अथासने दृढे योगी वशी हितमिताशनः।
गुरूपदिष्टमार्गेण प्राणायामान्समभ्यसेत्॥ १॥

1. Posture becoming established, a Yogī, master of himself, eating salutary and moderate food, should practise prāṇāyāma, as instructed by his guru.

चले वाते चलं चित्तं निश्चले निश्चलं भवेत्।
योगी स्थाणुत्वमाप्नोति ततो वायुं निरोधयेत्॥ २॥

2. Respiration being disturbed, the mind becomes disturbed. By restraining respiration, the Yogī gets steadiness of mind.

यावद्वायुः स्थितो देहे तावज्जीवनमुच्यते।
मरणं तस्य निष्क्रांतिस्ततो वायुं निरोधयेत्॥ ३॥

3. So long as the (breathing) air stays in the body, it is called life. Death consists in the passing out of the (breathing) air. It is, therefore, necessary to restrain the breath.

मलाकुलासु नाडीषु मारुतो नैव मध्यगः।
कथं स्यादुन्मनीभावः कार्यसिद्धिः कंथ भवेत्॥ ४॥

4. The breath does not pass through the middle channel (suṣumnā), owing to the impurities of the nāḍīs. How can then success be attained, and how can there be the unmanī avasthā.

शुद्धिमेति यदा सर्वं नाडीचक्रं मलाकुलम्।
तदैव जायते योगी प्राणसंग्रहणे क्षमः॥ ५॥

5. When the whole system of nāḍīs which is full of impurities, is cleaned, then the Yogī becomes able to control the Prāṇa.

प्राणायामं ततः कुर्यान्नित्यं सात्विकया धिया।
यथा सुषुम्नानाडीस्था मलाः शुद्धिं प्रयांति च॥ ६॥

6. Therefore, Prāṇāyāma should be performed daily with sātvika buddhi (intellect free from raja and tama or activity and sloth), in order to drive out the impurities of the suṣumnā.

बद्धपद्मासनो योगी प्राणं चंद्रेण पूरयेत्।
धारयित्वा यथाशक्ति भूयः सूर्येण रेचयेत्॥ ७॥
प्राणं सूर्येण चाकृष्यपूरयेदुदरं शनैः।
विधिवत्कुंभकं कृत्वा पुनश्चंद्रेण रेचयेत्॥ ८॥

Method of performing Prāṇāyāma

7–8. Sitting in the Padmāsana posture the Yogī should fill in the air through the left nostril (closing the right one); and, keeping it confined according to one's ability, it should be expelled slowly through the sūrya (right nostril). Then, drawing in the air through the sūrya (right nostril) slowly, the belly should be filled, and after performing Kumbhaka as before, it should be expelled slowly through the candra (left nostril).

येन त्यजेत्तेन पीत्वा धारयेदतिरोधतः।
रेचयेच्च ततोऽन्येन शनैरेव न वेगतः॥ ९॥

9. Inhaling thus through the one, through which it was expelled, and having restrained it there, till possible, it should be exhaled through the other, slowly and not forcibly.

प्राणं चेदिडया पिबेन्नियमितं भूयोऽन्यया रेचयेत्।
पीत्वा पिंगलया समीरणमथो बध्वात्यजेद्वामया।
सूर्याचंद्रमसोरनेन विधिनाभ्यासं सदा तन्वतां
शुद्धा नाडिगणा भवंतिं यमिनां मासत्रयादूर्ध्वतः॥ १०॥

10. If the air be inhaled through the left nostril, it should be expelled again through the other, and filling it through the right nostril, confining it there, it should be expelled through the left nostril. By practising in this way, through the right and the left nostrils alternately, the whole of the collection of the nāḍīs of the yamīs (practisers) becomes clean, *i.e.*, free from impurities, after 3 months and over.

प्रातर्मध्यंदिने सायमर्धरात्रे च कुंभकान्।
शनैरशीतिपर्यंतं चतुर्वारं समभ्यसेत्॥ ११॥

11. Kumbhakas should be performed gradually 4 times during day and night, *i.e.*, (morning, noon, evening and midnight), till the number of Kumbhakas for one time is 80 and for day and night together it is 320.

कनीयसि भवेत्स्वेद कंपो भवति मध्यमे।
उत्तमे स्थानमाप्नोति ततो वायुं निबंधयेत्॥ १२॥

12. In the beginning there is perspiration, in the middle stage there is quivering, and in the last or the 3rd stage one obtains steadiness; and then the breath should be made steady or motionless.

जलेन श्रमजातेन गात्रमर्दनमाचरेत्।
दृढता लघुता चैव तेन गात्रस्य जायते॥ १३॥

13. The perspiration exuding from exertion of practice should be rubbed into the body (and not wiped), as by so doing the body becomes strong.

अभ्यासकाले प्रथमे शस्तं क्षीराज्यभोजनम्।
ततोऽभ्यसे दृढीभूते न तादृङ् नियमग्रहः॥ १४॥

14. During the first stage of practice the food consisting of milk and ghee is wholesome. When the practice becomes established, no such restriction is necessary.

यथा सिंहो गजो व्याघ्रो भवेद्वश्यः शनैः शनैः।
तथैव सेवितो वायुरन्यथा हंति साधकम्॥ १५॥

15. Just as lions, elephants and tigers are controlled by and by, so the breath is controlled by slow degrees, otherwise (*i.e.,* by being hasty or using too much force) it kills the practiser himself.

प्राणायामादियुक्तेन सर्वरोगक्षयो भवेत्।
अयुक्ताभ्यासयोगेन सर्वरोगसमुद्भवः॥ १६॥

16. When Prāṇāyāma, etc., are performed properly, they eradicate all diseases; but an improper practice generates diseases.

हिक्का श्वासश्च कासश्च शिरःकर्णाक्षिवेदनाः।
भवंति विविधा रोगाः पवनस्य प्रकोपतः॥ १७॥

17. Hiccough, asthma, cough, pain in the head, the ears, and the eyes; these and other various kinds of diseases are generated by the disturbance of the breath.

युक्तं युक्तं त्यजेद्वायुं युक्तं च पूरयेत्।
युक्तं युक्तं च बध्नीयादेवं सिद्धिमवाप्नुयात्॥ १८॥

18. The air should be expelled with proper tact and should be filled in skilfully; and when it has been kept confined properly it brings success.

N.B.—The above caution is necessary to warn the aspirants against omitting any instruction; and, in their zeal to gain success or siddhis early, to begin the practice, either by using too much force in filling in, confining and expelling the air, or by omitting any instructions, it may cause unnecessary pressure on their ears, eyes, etc., and cause pain. Every word in the instructions is full of meaning and is necessarily used in the ślokas, and should be followed very carefully and with due attention. Thus there will be nothing to fear whatsoever. We are inhaling and exhaling the air throughout our lives without any sort of danger, and Prāṇāyāma being only a regular form of it, there should be no cause to fear.

यदा तु नाडीशुद्धिः स्यात्तथा चिह्नानि बाह्यतः।
कायस्य कृशता कांतिस्तदा जायेत निश्चितम्॥ १९॥

19. When the nāḍīs become free from impurities, and there appear the outward signs of success, such as lean body and glowing colour, then one should feel certain of success.

यथेष्टधारणं वायोरनलस्य प्रदीपनम्।
नादाभिव्यक्तिरारोग्यं जायते नाडीशोधनात्॥ २०॥

20. By removing the impurities, the air can be restrained, according to one's wish and the appetite is increased, the divine sound is awakened, and the body becomes healthy.

मेदश्लेष्माधिकः पूर्वं षट् कर्माणि समाचरेत्।
अन्यस्तु नाचरेत्तानि दोषाणां समभावतः॥ २१॥

21. If there be excess of fat or phlegm in the body, the six kinds of kriyās (duties) should be performed first. But others, not suffering from the excess of these, should not perform them.

धौतिर्बस्तिस्तथा नेतिस्त्राटकं नौलिकं तथा।
कपालभातिश्चैतानि षट् कर्माणि प्रचक्षते॥ २२॥

22. The six kinds of duties are : Dhauti, Basti, Neti, Trāṭaka, Nauli and Kapāla Bhāti. These are called the six actions

षट्कर्म.

कर्मषट्कमिदं गोप्यं घटशोधनकारकम्।
विचित्रगुणसंधायि पूज्यते योगिपुंगवैः॥ २३॥

23. These six kinds of actions which cleanse the body should be kept secret. They produce extraordinary attributes and are performad with earnestness by the best of Yogīs.

तत्र धौतिः

चतुरंगुलविस्तारं हस्तपंचदशायतम्।
गुरूपदिष्टमार्गेण सिक्तं वस्त्रं शनैर्ग्रसेत्।
पुनः प्रत्याहरेच्चैतदुदितं धौतिकर्म तत्॥ २४॥

The Dhauti (**धौति**)

24. A strip of cloth, about 3 inches wide and 15 cubits long, is pushed in (swallowed); when moist with warm water, through the passage shown by the *guru,* and is taken out again, This is called Dhauti Karma.

N.B.—The strip should be moistened with a little warm water, and the end should be held with the teeth. It is swallowed slowly, little by little; thus, first day 1 cubit, 2nd day 2 cubits, 3rd day 3 cubits, and so on. After swallowing it the stomach should be given a good, rouud motion from left to right, and then it should be taken out slowly and gently.

कासश्वासप्लीहकुष्ठं कफरोगांश्च विंशतिः।
धौतिकर्मप्रभावेन प्रयांत्येव न संशयः॥ २५॥

25. There is no doubt, that cough, asthma, enlargement of the spleen, leprosy, and 20 kinds of diseases born of phlegm, disappear by the practice of Dhauti Karma.

नाभिदघ्नजले पायौ न्यस्तनालोत्कटासनः।
आधाराकुंचनं कुर्यात्क्षालनं बस्तिकर्म तत्॥ २६॥

The Basti (**बस्तिकर्म**)

26. Squatting in navel-deep water, and introducing a six inches long, smooth piece of ½ an inch diameter pipe, open at both ends, half inside the anus; it (anus) should be drawn up (contracted) and then expelled. This washing is called the Basti Karma.

गुल्मप्लीहोदरं चापि वातपित्तकफोद्भवाः।
बस्तिकर्मप्रभावेन क्षीयंते सकलामयाः॥ २७॥

27. By practising this Basti Karma, colic, enlarged spleen, and dropsy, arising from the disorders of Vāta (air), Pitta (bile) and Kapha (phlegm), are all cured.

धात्विंद्रियांतःकरणप्रसादं
दद्याच्च कांतिंदहनप्रदीप्तिम्।
अशेषदोषोपचयं निहन्यात्
दभ्यस्यमानं जलबस्तिकर्म॥ २८॥

28. By practising Basti with water, the Dhātus, the Indriyas and the mind become calm. It gives glow and tone to the body and increases the appetite. All the disorders disappear.

अथ नेतिः

सूत्रं वितस्ति सुस्निग्धं नासानाले प्रवेशयेत्।
मुखान्निर्गम येच्चैषा नेतिः सिद्धैर्निगद्यते॥ २९॥

The Neti (नेति)

29. A cord made of threads and about six inches long, should be passed through the passage of the nose and the end taken out in the mouth. This is called by adepts the Neti Karma.

कपालशोधिनी चैव दिव्यदृष्टिप्रदायिनी।
जत्रूर्ध्वजातरोगौघं नेतिराशु निहंति च॥ ३०॥

30. The Neti is the cleaner of the brain and giver of divine sight. It soon destroys all the diseases of the cervical and scapular regions.

अथ त्राटकं

निरीक्षेन्निश्चलदृशा सूक्ष्मलक्ष्यं समाहितः।
अश्रुसंपातपर्यंत माचार्यैस्त्राटकं स्मृतम्॥ ३१॥

The Trāṭaka (त्राटक)

31. Being calm, one should gaze steadily at a small mark, till eyes are filled with tears. This is called Trāṭaka by ācāryas.

मोचनं नेत्ररोगाणां तंद्रादीनां कपाटकम्।
यत्नतस्त्राटकं गोप्यं यथा हाटकपेटकम्॥ ३२॥

32. Trāṭaka destroys the eye diseases and removes sloth, etc. It should be kept secret very carefully, like a box of jewellery.

अथ नौलिः

अमंदावर्तवेगेन तुंदं सव्यापसव्यतः।
नतांसो भ्रामयेदेषा नौलिः सिद्धैः प्रचक्ष्यते॥ ३३॥

The Nauli (नौलि)

33. Sitting on the toes with heels raised above the ground, and the palms resting on the ground, and in this bent posture the belly is moved forcibly from left to right just, as in vomiting. This is called by adepts the Nauli Karma.

मंदाग्निसंदीपनपाचनादि
संधापिका नंदकरी सदैव।
अशेष दोषामयशोषणी च
हठक्रियामौलिरियं च नौलिः॥ ३४॥

34. It removes dyspepsia, increases appetite and digestion, and is like the goddess of creation, and causes happiness. It dries up all the disorders. This Nauli is an excellent exercise in Haṭha Yoga.

अथ कपालभातिः

भस्त्रावल्लोहकारस्य रेचपूरौ ससंभ्रमौ।
कपालभातिर्विख्याता कफदोषविशोषणी॥ ३५॥

The Kapāla Bhāti (कपाल भाति)

35. When inhalation and exhalation are performed very quickly, like a pair of bellows of a blacksmith, it dries up all the disorders from the excess of phlegm, and is known as Kapāla Bhāti.

षट्कर्मनिर्गतस्थौल्यकफदोषमलादिकः।
प्राणायामं ततः कुर्यादनायासेन सिद्ध्यति॥ ३६॥

36. When Prāṇāyāma is performed after getting rid of obesity born of the defects phlegm, by the performance of the six duties, it easily brings success.

प्राणायामैरेव सर्वे प्रशुष्यंति मला इति।
आचार्याणां तु केषांचिदन्यत्कर्म न संमतम्॥ ३७॥

37. Some ācāryas (teachers) do not advocate any other practice, being of opinion that all the impurities are dried up by the practice of Prāṇāyāma.

अथ गजकरणि

उदर गतपदार्थमुद्वमंति
पवनमपानमुदीर्य कंठनाले।
क्रमपरिचय वश्यनाडिचक्रा
गजकरणीति निगद्यते हठज्ञैः॥ ३८॥

Gaja Karaṇi (गजकरणि)

38. By carrying the Apāna Vāyu up to the throat, the food, etc., in the stomach are vomited. By degrees, the system of Nāḍīs (Śaṅkhinī) becomes known. This is called in Haṭha as Gaja Karaṇi.

ब्रह्मादयोऽपि त्रिदशाः पवनाभ्यास तत्पराः।
अभूवन्नंतकभयात्तस्मात्पवन मभ्यसेत्॥ ३९॥

39. Brahmā and other Devas were always engaged in the exercise of Prāṇāyāma, and, by means of it, got rid of the fear of death. Therefore, one should practise prāṇāyāma regularly.

यावद्बद्धो मरुद्देहे यावच्चित्तं निराकुलम्।
यावद्दृष्टिर्भ्रुवोर्मध्ये तावत्कालभयं कुतः॥ ४०॥

40. So long as the breath is restrained in the body, so long as the mind is undisturbed, and so long as the gaze is fixed between the eyebrows, there is no fear from Death.

विधिवत्प्राणसंयामैर्नाडीचक्रे विशोधिते।
सुषुम्नावदनं भित्वा सुखाद्विशति मारुतः॥ ४१॥

41. When the system of Nāḍīs becomes clear of the impurities by properly controlling the prāṇa, then the air, piercing the entrance of the Suṣumnā enters it easily.

अथ मनोन्मनी

मारुते मध्यसंचारे मनःस्थैर्यं प्रजायते।
यो मनःसुस्थिरीभावः सैवावस्था मनोन्मनी॥ ४२॥

Manonmanī (मनोन्मनी)

42. Steadiness of mind comes when the air moves freely in the middle. That is the manonmanī (मनोन्मनी) condition, which is attained when the mind becomes calm.

तत्सिद्धये विधानज्ञाश्चित्रान्कुर्वंति कुंभकान्।
विचित्रकुंभकाभ्यासाद्विचित्रां सिद्धिमाप्नुयात्॥ ४३॥

43. To accomplish it, various Kumbhakas are performed by those who are expert in the methods; for, by the practice of different Kumbhakas, wonderful success is attained.

अथ कुंभकभेदाः

सूर्यभेदनमुज्जायी सीत्कारी सीतली तथा।
भस्त्रिका भ्रामरी मूर्च्छा प्लाविनीत्यष्ट कुंभकाः॥ ४४॥

Different kinds of Kumbhakas

44. Kumbhakas are of eight kinds, *viz.*, Sūrya

Bhedan, Ujjāyī, Sītkārī, Sītalī, Bhastrikā, Bhrāmarī, Mūrcchā, and Plāvinī.

पूरकांते तु कर्तव्यो बंधो जालंधराभिधः।
कुंभकांते रेचकादौ कर्तव्यस्तुड्डियानकः॥ ४५॥

45. At the end of Pūraka, Jālandhara Bandha should be performed, and at the end of Kumbhaka, and at the beginning of Recaka, Uḍḍiyāna Bandha should be performed.

N.B.—Pūraka is filling in of the air from outside.

Kumbhaka is the keeping the air confined inside. Recaka is expelling the confined air. The instructions for Pūraka, Kumbaka and Recaka will be found at their proper place and should be carefully followed.

अधस्तात्कुंचनेनाशु कंठसंकोचने कृते।
मध्ये पश्चिमतानेन स्याप्राणो ब्रह्मनाडिगः॥ ४६॥

46. By drawing up from below (Mūla Bandha) and contracting the throat (Jālandhara Bandha) and by pulling back the middle of the front portion of the body *(i.e.,* belly), the Prāṇa goes to the Brahma Nāḍī (Suṣumnā).

The middle hole, through the vertebral column, through which the spinal cord passes, is called the Suṣumnā Nāḍī of the Yogīs. The two other sympathetic cords, one on each side of the spinal cord, are called the Iḍā and the Piṅgalā Nāḍīs. These will be described later on.

आपानमूर्ध्वमुत्थाप्य प्राणं कंठादधो नयेत्।
योगी जराविमुक्तः सन् षोडशाब्दवयो भवेत्॥ ४७॥

47. By pulling up the Apāna Vāyu and by forcing the Prāṇa Vāyu down the throat, the Yogī, liberated from old age, becomes young, as it were 16 years old.

Note.—**हृदि प्राणो गुदेऽपानः समानो नाभिमण्डले।**
उदानः कण्ठदेशस्थो व्यानः सर्वशरीरगः।

The seat of the Prāṇa is the heart; of the Apāna anus; of the

Samāna the region about the navel; of the Udāna the throat; while the Vyāna moves throughout the body.

अथ सूर्यभेदनं

आसने सुखदे योगी बध्वा चैवासनं ततः।
दक्षनाड्या समाकृष्य बहिःस्थं पवनं शनैः॥ ४८॥

Sūrya Bhedana (**सूर्य भेदन**)

48. Taking any comfortable posture and performing the āsana, the Yogī should draw in the air slowly, through the right nostril.

आकेशादानखाग्राच्च निरोधावधि कुंभयेत्।
ततः शनैः सव्यनाड्या रेचयेत्पवनं शनैः॥ ४९॥

49. Then it should be confined within, so that it fills from the nails to the tips of the hair, and then let out through the left nostril slowly.

Note.—This is to be done alternately with both the nostrils, drawing in through the one, expelling through the other and *vice versa.*

कपालशोधनं वातदोषघ्नं कृतिदोषहृत्।
पुनः पुनरिदं कार्यं सूर्यभेदनमुत्तमम्॥ ५०॥

50. This excellent Sūrya Bhedana cleanses the forehead (frontal sinuses), destroys the disorders of Vāta, and removes the worms, and, therefore, it should be performed again and again.

Note— योगाभ्यास क्रमं वक्ष्ये योगिनां योगसिद्धये।
उषःकाले समुत्थाय प्रातःकालेऽथवा बुधः॥ १॥
गुरुं संस्मृत्य शिरसि हृदये स्वेष्टदेवताम्।
शौचंकृत्वा दन्तशुद्धिं विदध्याद् भस्मधारणम्॥ २॥
शुचौ देशे मठे रम्ये प्रतिष्ठाप्यासनं मृदु।
तत्रोपविश्य संस्मृत्य मनसा गुरुमीश्वरम्॥ ३॥
देशकालौ च संकीर्त्य संकल्प्य विधिपूर्वकम्।
अद्येत्यादि श्रीपरमेश्वरप्रसादपूर्वकं समाधि तत्फल
सिद्ध्यर्थमासनपूर्वकान् प्राणायामादीन् करिष्ये।

अनंतं प्रणमेद्देवं नागेशं पीठसिद्धये॥ ४॥
मणिभ्रात्फणासहस्रविधृतविश्वंभरामंडलायानंताय नागराजायनमः।
ततोभ्यसेदासनानि श्रमे जाते शवासनम्।
अन्ते समभ्यसे त्तत्तु श्रमाभावे तु नाभ्यसेत्॥ ५॥
करणीं विपरीताख्यां कुंभकात्पूर्वमभ्यसेत्।
जालंधर प्रसादार्थं कुम्भकात्पूर्वयोगतः॥ ६॥
विधायामचनं कृत्वा कर्मांगं प्राणसंयमम्।
योगींद्रादीन्नमस्कृत्य कौर्म्मीञ्च शिववाक्यतः॥ ७॥
कूर्म पुराणे।
नमस्कृत्याथ योगींद्रान् सशिष्यांच्च विनायकम्।
गुरुंचैवाथमां योगी युंजीत सुसमाहितः॥ ८॥
बद्धाभ्यासे सिद्धपीठं कुम्भकाबंधपूर्वकम्।
प्रथमे दशकर्तव्या पंचवृद्ध्या दिने दिने॥ ९॥
कार्या अशीति पर्यंतं कुम्भकाः सुसमाहितैः।
योगींद्रः प्रथमं कुर्यादभ्यासं चंद्रसूर्ययोः॥ १०॥
अनुलोमविलोमाख्य मेतं प्राहुर्मनीषिणः।
सूर्यभेदनमभ्यस्य बंधपूर्वकमेकधीः॥ ११॥
उज्जायिनं ततः कुर्यात्सीत्कारीं शीतलीं ततः।
भस्त्रिकांच समभ्यस्य कुर्यादन्यान्नवापरान्॥ १२॥
मुद्राः समभ्यसेद्बद्ध गुरु वक्त्राद् यथाक्रमम्।
ततः पद्मासनं बद्ध्वा कुर्यन्नादानुचिंतनम्॥ १३॥
अभ्यासं सकलं कुर्यादीश्वरार्पणमादृतः।
अभ्यासादुत्थितः स्नानं कुर्यादुष्णेन वारिणा॥ १४॥
स्नात्वा समापयेन्नित्यं कर्म संक्षेपतः सुधीः।
मध्याह्नेपितथाभ्यस्य किञ्चिद्विश्रम्य भोजनम्॥ १५॥
कुर्वीत योगिनां पथ्यमपथ्यन्नकदाचन।
एलांवापि लवंगंवा भोजनान्ते च भक्षयेत्॥ १६॥
केचित्कर्पूरमिच्छंति तांबूलं शोभनं तथा।
चूर्णेन रहितं शस्तं पवनाभ्यासयोगिनाम्॥ १७॥
भोजनानंतरंकुर्यान्मोक्षशास्त्रावलोकनम्।
पुराणश्रवणंवापि नाम संकीर्तनं विभोः॥ १८॥
सायं संध्याविधिं कृत्वायोगं पूर्ववदभ्यसेत्।
यदा त्रिघटिका शेषो दिवसोऽभ्यासमाचरेत्॥ १९॥
अभ्यासानंतरंकार्या सायंसंध्या सदा बुधैः।
अर्धरात्रे हठाभ्यासं विदध्यात्पूर्ववद्यमी॥ २०॥
विपरीतां तु करणीं सायंकालार्धरात्रयोः।
नाभ्यसेद्भोजनादूर्ध्वं यतः सा न प्रशस्यते॥ २१॥

Translation : I am going to describe the procedure of the practice of Yoga, in order that Yogīs may succeed, A wise man should leave his bed in the Uṣā Kāla. (*i.e.*, at the peep of dawn or

4 o'clock) in the morning.

Remembering his guru over his head, and his desired deity in his heart, after answering the calls of nature, and cleaning his mouth, he should apply Bhasma (ashes).

In a clean spot, clean room and charming ground, he should spread a soft āsana (cloth for sitting on). Having seated on it and remembering in his mind his guru and his God.

Having extolled the place and the time and taking up the vow thus: 'To day by the grace of God, I will perform Prāṇāyāmas with āsanas for gaining samādhi (trance) and its fruits.' He should salute the infinite Deva, Lord of the Nāgas, to ensure success in the āsanas (postures).

Salutation to the Lord of the Nāgas, who is adorned with thousands of heads, set with brilliant jewels (maṇis), and who has sustained the whole universe, nourishes it, and is infinite. After this he should begin his exercise of āsanas and when fatigued, he should practise Śava āsana. Should there be no fatigue, he should not practise it.

Before Kumbhaka, he should perform Viparīta Karṇī mudrā, in order that he may be able to perform Jālandhara bandha comfortably.

Sipping a little water, he should begin the exercise of Prāṇāyāma, after saluting Yogīndras, as described in the Kūrma Purāṇa, in the words of Śiva.

Such as "Saluting Yogīndras and their disciples and guru Vināyaka, the Yogī should unite with me with composed mind."

While practising, he should sit with Siddhāsana, and having performed *bandha* and Kumbhaka, should begin with10 Prāṇāyāmas the first day, and go on increasing 5 daily.

With composed mind 80 Kumbhakas should be performed at a time; beginning first with the candra (the left nostril) and then sūrya (the right nostril).

This has been spoken of by wise men as Anuloma and Viloma, Having practised Sūrya Bhedana, with Bandhas, the wise man should practise Ujjāyī and then Sītkārī Śītalī, and Bhastrikā, he may practice others or not.

He should practise mudrās properly, as instructed by his guru. Then sitting with Padmāsana, he should hear anāhata nāda attentively.

He should *resign the fruits of all his practice reverently to God,* and, on rising on the completion of the practice, a warm bath should be taken.

The bath should bring all the daily duties briefly to an end. At noon also a little rest should be taken at the end of the exercise, and then food should be taken.

Yogīs should always take wholesome food and never anything unwholesome. After dinner he should eat ilācī or lavaṅga.

Some like camphor, and betel leaf. To the Yogīs, practising Prāṇāyāma, betel leaf without powders, *i.e.,* lime, nuts and kātha, is beneficial.

After taking food he should read books treating of salvation, or hear Purāṇas and repeat the name of God.

In the evening the exercise should be begun after finishing sandhyā, as before, beginning the practice 3 ghaṭikā or one hour before the sun sets.

Evening sandhyā should always be performed after practice, and Haṭha Yoga should be practised at midnight.

Viparīta Karṇi is to be practised in the evening and at midnight, and not just after eating, as it does no good at this time.

अथोज्जायी

मुखं संयम्य नाडीभ्यामाकृष्य पवनं शनैः।
यथा लगति कंठात्तु हृदयावधि सस्वनम्॥ ५१॥

Ujjāyī (**उज्जाई**)

51. Having closed the opening of the Nāḍī (Larynx), the air should be drawn in such a way that it goes touching from the throat to the chest, and making noise while passing.

पूर्ववत्कुंभयेत्प्राणं रेचयेदिडया ततः॥
श्लेष्मदोषहरं कंठे देहानलविवर्धनम्॥ ५२॥

52. It should be restrained, as before, and then let out through Iḍā (the left nostril). This removes śleṣma (phlegm) in the throat and increases the appetite.

नाडीजलोदराधातुगतदोषविनाशनम्।
गच्छता तिष्ठता कार्यमुज्जाय्याख्यं तु कुंभकम्॥ ५३॥

53. It destroys the defects of the nāḍīs, dropsy and disorders of Dhātu (humours). Ujjāyī should be performed in all conditions of life, even while walking or sitting.

अथ सीत्कारी

सीत्कां कुर्यात्तथा वक्त्रे घ्राणेनैव विजृंभिकाम्॥
एवमभ्यासयोगेन कामदेवो द्वितीयकः॥ ५४॥

Sītkārī (**सीत्कारी**)

54. Sītkārī is performed by drawing in the air through the mouth, keeping the tongue between the lips. The air thus drawn in should not be expelled through the mouth. By practising in this way, one becomes next to the God of Love in beauty.

योगिनीचक्रसामान्यः सृष्टिसंहारकारकः।
न क्षुधा न तृषा निद्रा नैवालस्यं प्रजायते॥ ५५॥

55. He is regarded adorable by the Yoginīs and becomes the destroyer of the cycle of creation. He is not afflicted with hunger, thirst, sleep or lassitude.

भवेत्सत्वं च देहस्य सर्वोपद्रववर्जितः।
अनेन विधिना सत्यं योगींद्रो भूमिमंडले॥ ५६॥

56. The Satva of his body becomes free from all the disturbances. In truth, he becomes the lord of the Yogīs in this world.

अथ शीतली

जिह्वया वायुमाकृष्य पूर्ववत्कुंभसाधनम्।
शनकैर्घ्राणरंध्राभ्यां रेचयेत्पवनं सुधीः॥ ५७॥

Śītalī (**शीतली**)

57. As in the above (Sītkāri), the tongue to be protruded a little out of the lips, when the air is drawn in. It is kept confined, as before, and then expelled slowly through the nostrils.

गुल्मप्लीहादिकान् रोगान् ज्वरं पित्तं क्षुधां तृषाम्।
विषाणि शीतलीनाम कुंभिकेयं निहंति हि॥ ५८॥

58. This Śītalī Kumbhikā cures colic, (enlarged) spleen, fever, disorders of bile, hunger, thirst, and counteracts poisons.

अथ भस्त्रिका

ऊर्वोरुपरि संस्थाप्य शुभे पादतले उभे।
पद्मासनं भवेदेतत्सर्वपापप्रणाशनम्॥ ५९॥

The Bhastrikā (भस्त्रिका)

59. The Padma Āsana consists in crossing the feet and placing them on both the thighs; it is the destroyer of all sins.

सम्यक् पद्मासनं बध्वा समग्रीवोदरं सुधीः।
मुखं संयम्य यत्नेन घ्राणं घ्राणेन रेचयेत्॥ ६०॥

60. Binding the PadmaĀsana and keeping the body straight, closing the mouth carefully, let the air be expelled through the nose.

यथा लगति हृत्कंठे कपालावधि सस्वनम्।
वेगेन पूरयेच्चापि हृत्पद्मावधि मारुतम्॥ ६१॥

61. It should be filled up to the lotus of the heart, by drawing it in with force, making noise and touching the throat, the chest and the head.

पुनर्विरेचयेत्तद्वत्पूरयेच्च पुनः पुनः।
यथैव लोहकारेण भस्त्रा वेगेन चाल्यते॥ ६२॥

62. It should be expelled again and filled again and again as before, just as a pair of bellows of the blacksmith is worked.

तथैव स्वशरीरस्थं चालयेत्पवनं धिया।
यदा श्रमो भवेद्देहे तदा सूर्येण पूरयेत्॥ ६३॥

63. In the same way, the air of the body should be moved intelligently, filling it through Sūrya when fatigue is experienced.

यथोदरं भवेत्पूर्णमनिलेन तथा लघु।
धारयेन्नासिकां मध्यतर्जनीभ्यां विना दृढम्॥ ६४॥

64. The air should be drawn in through the right nostril by pressing the thumb against the left side of the nose, so as to close the left nostril; and when filled to the full, it should be closed with the fourth finger (the one next to the little finger) and kept confined.

विधिवत्कुंभकं कृत्वा रेचयेदिडयानिलम्।
वातपित्तश्लेष्महरं शरीराग्निविवर्धनम्॥ ६५॥

65. Having confined it properly, it should be expelled through the Iḍā (left nostril). This destroys vāta, pitta (bile) and phlegm and increases the digestive power (the gastric fire).

कुंडलीबोधकं पवनं क्षिप्रंसुखदं हितम्।
ब्रह्मनाडीमुखेसंस्थकफाद्यर्गलनाशनम्॥ ६६॥

66. It quickly awakens the Kuṇḍalinī, purifies the system, gives pleasure, and is beneficial. It destroys phlegm and the impurities accumulated at the entrance of the Brahma Nāḍī.

सम्यग्गात्रसमुद्भूत् ग्रंथित्रयविभेदकम्।
विशेषेणैव कर्तव्यं भस्त्राख्यं कुंभकं त्विदम्॥ ६७॥

67. This Bhastrikā should be performed plentifully, for it breaks the three knots : Brahma granthi (in the chest), Viṣṇu granthi (in the throat), and Rudra granthi (between the eyebrows) of the body.

अथ भ्रामरी

वेगाद्घोषं पूरकं भृंगनादं
भृंगीनादं रेचकं मंदमंदम्।
योगींद्राणामेवमभ्यासयोगाच्चित्ते
जाता काचिदानंदलीला॥ ६८॥

Tke Bhrāmarī (**भ्रामरी**)

68. By filling the air with force, making noise like Bhṛṅgī (wasp), and expelling it slowly, making noise in the same way; this practice causes a sort of ecstacy in the minds of Yogīndras.

अथ मूर्च्छा

पूरकांते गाढतरं बध्वाजालंधरंशनैः।
रेचयेन्मूर्छनाख्येयं मनोमूर्छा सुखप्रदा॥ ६९॥

The Mūrcchā (मूर्च्छा)

69. Closing the passages with Jālandhara Bandha firmly at the end of Pūraka, and expelling the air slowly, is called Mūrcchā, from its causing the mind to swoon and giving comfort.

अथ प्लाविनी

अंतः प्रवर्तितोदारमारुतापूरितोदरः।
पयस्यगाधेऽपिसुखात्प्लवते पद्मपत्रवत्॥ ७०॥

The Plāvinī (प्लाविनी)

70. When the belly is filled with air and the inside of the body is filled to its utmost with air, the body floats on the deepest water, like the leaf of a lotus.

प्राणायामस्त्रिधा प्रोक्तो रेचपूरककुंभकैः।
सहितः केवलश्चेति कुंभको द्विविधो मतः॥ ७१॥

71. Considering Pūraka (filling), Recaka (expelling) and Kumbhaka (confining), Prāṇāyāma is of three kinds, but considering it accompanied by Pūraka and Recaka, and without these, it is of two kinds only, *i.e.*, Sahita (with) and Kevala,(alone).

यावत्केवलसिद्धिः स्यात्सहितं तावदभ्यसेत्।
रेचकं पूरकं मुक्त्वा सुखं यद्वायुधारणम्॥ ७२॥

72. Exercise in Sahita should be continued till success in Kevala is gained. This latter is simply confining the air with ease, without Recaka and Pūraka.

प्राणायामोऽयमित्युक्तः स वै केवलकुंभकः।
कुंभके केवले सिद्धे रेचपूरकवर्जिते॥ ७३॥

73. In the practice of Kevala Prāṇāyāma when it can he performed successfully without Recaka and Pūraka, then it is called Kevala Kumbhaka.

न तस्य दुर्लभं किंचित्त्रिषु लोकेषु विद्यते।
शक्तः केवलकुंभेन यथेष्टं वायुधारणात्॥ ७४॥

74. There is nothing in the three worlds which may be difficult to obtain for him who is able to keep the air confined according to pleasure, by means of Kevala Kumbhaka.

राजयोगपदं चापि लभते नात्रसंशयः।
कुंभकात्कुंडलीबोधः कुंडलीबोधतो भवेत्॥ ७५॥

75. He obtains the position of Rāja Yoga undoubtedly. Kuṇḍalinī awakens by Kumbhaka, and by its awakening. Suṣumnā becomes free from impurities.

अनर्गला सुषुम्ना च हठसिद्धिश्च जायते।
हठं विना राजयोगो राजयोगं विना हठः।
न सिध्याति ततो युग्ममानिष्पत्तेः समभ्यसेत्॥ ७६॥

76. No success in Rāja Yoga without Haṭha Yoga, and no success in Haṭha Yoga without Rāja Yoga. One should, therefore, practise both of these well, till complete success is gained.

कुंभकप्राणरोधांते कुर्याश्चित्तं निराश्रयम्।
एवमभ्यासयोगेन राजयोगपदं व्रजेत्॥ ७७॥

77. On the completion of Kumbhaka, the mind should be given rest. By practising in this way one is raised to the position of (succeeds in getting) Rāja Yoga.

वपुः कृशत्वं वदनेप्रसन्नता
नादस्फुटत्वं नयने सुनिर्मले।
अरोगता बिंदुजयोऽग्निदीपनं
नाडीविशुद्धिर्हठयोगलक्षणम्॥ ७८॥

Indications of success in the practice of Haṭha Yoga.

78. When the body becomes lean, the face glows with delight, Anāhata-nāda manifests, and eyes are clear, body is healthy, *bindu* under control, and appetite increases, then one should know that the Nāḍīs are purified and success in Haṭha Yoga is approaching.

इति हठप्रदीपिकायां द्वितीयोपदेशः॥ २॥

End of Chapter II, On Prāṇāyāma

Chapter III

तृतीयोपदेशः

On Mudrās

सशैलवनधात्रीणां यथाधारोऽहिनायकः।
सर्वेषां योगतंत्राणां तथाधारो हि कुंडली॥ १॥

1. As the chief of the snakes is the support of the earth with all the mountains and forests on it, so all the Tantras (Yoga practices) rest on the Kuṇḍalinī. (The Vertebral column).

सुप्ता गुरुप्रसादेन यदा जागर्ति कुंडली।
तदा सर्वाणि भिद्यंते ग्रंथयोऽपि च॥ २॥

2. When the sleeping Kuṇḍalinī awakens by favour of a *guru*, then all the lotuses (in the six cakras or centres) and all the knots are pierced through.

प्राणस्य शून्यपदवी तथा राजपथायते।
तदा चित्तं निरालंबं तदा कालस्य वंचनम्॥ ३॥

3. Suṣumnā (Śūnya Padavī) becomes a main road for the passage of Prāṇa, and the mind then becomes free from all connections (with its objects of enjoyments) and Death is then evaded.

सुषुम्ना शून्यपदवी ब्रह्मरंध्रं महापथः।
श्मशानं शांभवी मध्यमार्गश्चेत्येकवाचकाः॥ ४॥

4. Suṣumnā, Śūnya Padavī, Brahma Randhra,

Mahā Patha, Śmaśāna, Śambhavī, Madhya Mārga, are names of one and the same thing.

तस्मात्सर्वप्रयत्नेन प्रबोधयितुमीश्वरीम्।
ब्रह्मद्वारमुखे सुप्तां मुद्राभ्यासं समाचरेत्॥ ५॥

5. In order, therefore, to awaken this goddess, who is sleeping at the entrance of Brahma Dvāra (the great door), mudrās should be practised well.

अथ मुद्राभेदाः

महामुद्रा महाबंधो महावेधश्च खेचरी।
उड्यानं मूलबंधश्च बंधो जालंधराभिधः॥ ६॥

The Mudrās

6. Mahā Mudrā, Mahā Bandha, Mahā Vedha, Khecrī, Uḍḍiyāna Bandha, Mūla Bandha, Jālandhara Bandha.

करणी विपरीताख्या वज्रोली शक्तिचालनम्।
इदं हि मुद्रादशकं जरामरणनाशनम्॥ ७॥

7. Viparīta Karaṇī, Vajrolī and Śakti Cālana. These are the ten Mudrās which annihilate old age and death.

आदिनाथोदितं दिव्यमष्टैश्वर्यप्रदायकम्।
वल्लभं सर्वसिद्धानां दुर्लभं मारुतामपि॥ ८॥

8. They have been explained by Ādi Nātha (Śiva) and give eight kinds of divine wealth. They are loved by all the Siddhas and are hard to attain even by the Marutas.

Note—The eight *Aiśvaryas* are : Aṇimā (becoming small, like an atom), Mahimā (becoming great, like ākāśa, by drawing in atoms of Prakṛti), Garimā (light things, like cotton becoming very heavy like mountains).

Prāpti (coming within easy reach of everything; as touching the moon with the little finger, while standing on the earth).

Prākāmya (non-resistance to the desires, as entering the earth like water).

Īsatā (mastery over matter and objects made of it).
Vaśītva (controlling the animate and inanimate objects).

गापनीयं प्रयत्नेन यथा रत्नकरंडकम्।
कस्यचिन्नैव वक्तव्यं कुलस्त्रीसुरतं यथा॥ ९॥

9. These Mudrās should be kept secret by every means, as one keeps one's box of jewellery, and should, on no account be told to anyone, just as husband and wife keep their dealings secret.

अथ महामुद्रा
पादमूलेन वामेन योनिं संपीड्य दक्षिणां।
प्रसारितं पदं कृत्वा कराभ्यां धारये दृढम्॥ १०॥

The Mahā Mudrā

10. Pressing the Yoni (perineum) with the heel of the left foot, and stretching forth the right foot, its toe should he grasped by the thumb and first finger.

कंठे बंधं समारोप्य धारयेद्वायुमूर्ध्वतः।
यथा दण्डहतः सर्पो दंडाकारः प्रजायते॥ ११॥
ऋज्वीभूता तथा शक्तिः कुंडली सहसा भवेत्।
तदा सा मरणावस्था जायते द्विपुटाश्रया॥ १२॥

11–12. By stopping the throat (by Jālandhara Bandha) the air is drawn in from the outside and carried down. Just as a snake struck with a stick becomes straight like a stick, in the same way, *śakti* (Suṣumnā) becomes straight at once. Then the Kuṇḍalinī, becoming as it were dead, and, leaving both the Iḍā and the Piṅgalā, enters the Suṣumnā (the middle passage).

ततः शनैः शनैरेव रेचयेन्नैव वेगतः।
महामुद्रां च तेनैव वदन्ति विबुधोत्तमाः।
इयं खलु महामुद्रा महासिद्धैः प्रदर्शिता॥ १३॥

13. It should be expelled then, slowly only and not

violently. For this very reason, the best of the wise men call it the Mahā Mudrā. This Mahā Mudrā has been propounded by great masters.

महाक्लेशादयो दोषाः क्षीयंते मरणादयः।
महामुद्रां च तनैव वदंति विबुधोत्तमाः॥ १४॥

14. Great evils and pains, like death, are destroyed by it, and for this reason wise men call it the Mahā Mudrā.

चंद्रांगे तु समभ्यस्य सूर्यांगे पुनरभ्यसेत्।
यावत्तुल्या भवेत्संख्या ततो मुद्रां विसर्जयेत्॥ १५॥

15. Having practised with the left nostril, it should be practised with the right one; and, when the number on both sides becomes equal, then the mudrā should be discontinued.

नहि पथ्यमपथ्यं वा रसाः सर्वेऽपि नीरसाः।
अपि भुक्तं विषं घोरं पीयूषमपि जीर्यति॥ १६॥

16. There is nothing wholesome or injurious; for the practice of this mudrā destroys the injurious effects of all the rasas (chemicals). Even the deadliest of poisons, if taken, acts like nectar.

क्षयकुष्ठगुदावर्तगुल्माजीर्णपुरोगमाः।
तस्य दोषाः क्षयं यांति महामुद्रां तु योऽभ्यसेत्॥ १७॥

17. Consumption, leprosy, prolapsus anii, colic, and the diseases due to indigestion,—all these irregularities are removed by the practice of this Mahā Mudrā.

कथितेयं महामुद्रा महासिद्धिकरा नृणाम्।
गोपनीया प्रयत्नेन न देया यस्यकस्यचित्॥ १८॥

18. This Mahā Mudrā has been described as the giver of great success (Siddhi) to men. It should be kept secret by every effort, and not revealed to any and everyone.

अथ महाबंधः

पार्ष्णिं वामस्य पादस्य योनिस्थाने नियोजयेत्।
वामोरूपरि संस्थाप्य दक्षिणं चरणं तथा॥ १९॥

The Mahā Bandha

19. Press the left heel to the perineum and place the right foot on the left thigh.

पूरयित्वा ततो वायुं हृदये चुबुकं दृढम्।
निष्पीड्य वायुमाकुंच्य मनोमध्ये नियोजयेत्॥ २०॥

20. Fill in the air, keeping the chin firm against the chest, and, having pressed the air, the mind should be fixed on the middle of the eyebrows or in the Suṣumnā (the spine).

धारयित्वा यथाशक्ति रेचयेदनिलं शनैः।
सव्यांगे तु समभ्यस्य दक्षांगे पुनरभ्यसेत्॥ २१॥

21. Having kept it confined so long as possible, it should be expelled slowly. Having practised on the left side, it should be practised on the right side.

मतमत्र तु केषांचित्कंठबंधं विवर्जयेत्।
राजदंतस्थजिह्वाया बंधः शस्तो भवेदिति॥ २२॥

22. Some are of opinion that the closing of throat is not necessary here, for keeping the tongue pressed against the roots of the upper teeth makes a good bandha (stop).

अयं तु सर्वनाडीनामूर्ध्वं गतिनिरोधकः।
अयं खलु महाबंधो महासिद्धिप्रदायकः॥ २३॥

23. This stops the upward motion of all the Nāḍīs. Verily this Mahā Bandha is the giver of great Siddhis.

कालपाशमहाबंधविमोचनविचक्षणः।
त्रिवेणीसंगमं धत्ते केदारं प्रापयेन्मनः॥ २४॥

24. This Mahā Bandha is the most skilful means for cutting away the snares of death. It brings about the conjunction of the Triveṇī (Iḍā, Piṅgalā and Suṣumnā) and carries the mind to Kedār (the space between the eyebrows, which is the seat of Śiva).

रूपलावण्यसंपन्ना यथा स्त्री पुरुषं विना।
महामुद्रामहाबंधौ निष्फलौ वेधवर्जितौ॥ २५॥

25. As beauty and loveliness, do not avail a woman without husband, so the Mahā Mudrā and the Mahā-Bandha are useless without the Mahā Vedha.

अथ महावेधः
महाबंधस्थितो योगी कृत्वा पूरकमेकधीः।
वायूनां गतिमावृत्य निभृतं कंठमुद्रया॥ २६॥

The Mahā Vedha

26. Sitting with Mahā Bandha, the Yogī should fill in the air and keep his mind collected. The movements of the Vāyus (Prāṇa and Apāna) should be stopped by closing the throat.

समहस्तयुगो भूमौ स्फिचौ संताडयेच्छनैः।
पुटद्वयमतिक्रम्य वायुः स्फुरति मध्यगः॥ २७॥

27. Resting both the hands equally on the ground, he should raise himself a little and strike his buttocks against the ground gently. The air, leaving both the passages (Iḍā and Piṅgalā), starts into the middle one.

सोमसूर्याग्निसंबंधो जायते चामृताय वै।
मृतावस्था समुत्पन्ना ततो वायुं विरेचयेत्॥ २८॥

28. The union of the Iḍā and the Piṅgalā is effected, in order to bring about immortality. When the air becomes as it were dead (by leaving its course through the Iḍā and the Piṅgalā) (*i.e.,* when it has been kept confined), then it should be expelled.

महावेधोऽयमभ्यासान्महासिद्धिप्रदायकः।
वलीपलितवेपघ्नः सेव्यते साधकोत्तमैः॥ २९॥

29. The practice of this Mahā Vedha, the giver of

great Siddhis, destroys old age, grey hair, and shaking of the body, and therefore it is practised by the best masters.

एतत्त्रयं महागुह्यं जरामृत्युविनाशनम्।
वह्निवृद्धिकरं चैव ह्यणिमादिगुणप्रदम्॥ ३०॥

30. These Three are the great secrets. They are the destroyers of old age and death, increase the appetite, confer the accomplishments of Aṇimā, etc.

अष्टधा क्रियते चैव यामे यामे दिने दिने।
पुण्यसंभारसंधायि पापौघभिदुरं सदा।
सम्यक्शिक्षावतामेवं स्वल्पं प्रथमसाधनम्॥ ३१॥

31. They should be practised in 8 ways, daily and hourly. They increase collection of good actions and lessen the evil ones. People, instructed well, should begin their practice, little by little, first.

अथ खेचरी

कपालकुहरे जिह्वा प्रविष्टा विपरीतगा।
भ्रुवोरंतर्गता दृष्टिर्मुद्रा भवति खेचरी॥ ३२॥

The Khecarī

32. The Khecarī Mudrā is accomplished by thrusting the tongue into the gullet, by turning it over itself, and keeping the eyesight in the middle of the eyebrows.

छेदनचालनदोहैः कलां क्रमेण वर्धयेत्तावत्।
सा यावद्भ्रूमध्यं स्पृशति तदा खेचरीसिद्धिः॥ ३३॥

33. To accomplish this, the tongue is lengthened by cutting the fraenum linguae, moving, and pulling it. When it can touch the space between the eyebrows, then Khecarī can be accomplished.

स्नुहीपत्रनिभं शस्त्रं सुतीक्ष्णं स्निग्धनिर्मलम्।
समादाय ततस्तेन रोममात्रं समुच्छिनेत्॥ ३४॥

34. Taking a sharp, smooth, and clean instrument, of the shape of a cactus leaf, the fraenum of the tongue should be cut a little (as much as a hair's thickness), at a time.

ततः सैंधवपथ्याभ्यां चूर्णिताभ्यां प्रकर्षयेत्।
पुनः सप्तदिने प्राप्ते रोममात्रं समुच्छिनेत्॥ ३५॥

35. Then rock salt and yellow myrobalan (both powdered) should be rubbed in. On the 7th day, it should again be cut a hair's breadth.

एवं क्रमेण षण्मासं नित्यं युक्तः समाचरेत्।
षण्मासाद्रसनामूलशिलाबंधः प्रणश्यति॥ ३६॥

36. One should go on doing thus, regularly for six months. At the end of six months, the fraenum of the tongue will be completely cut.

कलां पराङ्मुखीं कृत्वा त्रिपथे परियोजयेत्।
सा भवेत्खेचरी मुद्रा व्योमचक्रं तदुच्यते॥ ३७॥

37. Turning the tongue upwards, it is fixed on the three ways (oesophagus, windpipe and palate). Thus it makes the Khecarī Mudrā, and is called the Vyoma Cakra.

रसना मूर्ध्वगां कृत्वा क्षणार्धमपि तिष्ठति।
विषैविर्मुच्यते योगी व्याधिमृत्युजरादिभिः॥ ३८॥

38. The Yogī who sits for a minute turning his tongue upwards, is saved from poisons, diseases, death, old age, etc.

न रोगो मरणं तंद्रा न निद्रा न क्षुधा तृषा।
न च मूर्च्छा भवेत्तस्य यो मुद्रां वेत्ति खेचरीम्॥ ३९॥

39. He who knows the Khecarī Mudrā is not afflicted with disease, death, sloth, sleep, hunger, thirst, and swooning.

पीड्यते न स रोगेण लिप्यते न च कर्मणा।
बाध्यते न स कालेन यो मुद्रां वेत्ति खेचरीम्॥ ४०॥

40. He who knows the Khecarī Mudrā, is not troubled by diseases, is not stained with karmas, and is not snared by time.

चित्तं चरति खे यस्माज्जिह्वा चरति खे गता।
तेनैषा खेचरी नाम मुद्रा सिद्धैर्निरूपिता॥ ४१॥

41. The Siddhas have devised this Khecarī Mudrā from the fact that the mind and the tongue reach ākāśa by its practice.

खेचर्या मुद्रितं येन विवरं लंबिकोर्ध्वतः।
न तस्य क्षरते बिंदुः कामिन्याश्लेषितस्य च॥ ४२॥

42. If the hole behind the palate be stopped with Khecarī by turning the tongue upwards, then bindu cannot leave its place even if a woman were embraced.

ऊर्ध्वजिह्वः स्थिरो भूत्वा सोमपानं करोति यः।
मासार्धेन न संदेहो मृत्युं जयति योगवित्॥ ४३॥

43. If the Yogī drinks Somarasa (juice) by sitting with the tongue turned backwards and mind concentrated, there is no doubt he conquers death within 15 days.

नित्यं सोमकलापूर्णं शरीरे यस्य योगिनः।
तक्षकेणापि दष्टस्य विषं तस्य न सर्पति॥ ४४॥

44. If the Yogī, whose body is full of Somarasa (juice), were bitten by Takṣaka (snake), its poison cannot permeate his body.

इंधनानि यथा वह्निस्तैलवर्त्ति च दीपकः।
तथा सोमकलापूर्णं देही देहं न मुंचति॥ ४५॥

45. As fire is inseparably connected with the wood and light is connected with the wick and oil, so does the soul not leave the body full of nectar exuding from the Soma.

Note—Soma (Candra) is described later on located in the thousand-petalled lotus in the human brain, and is the same as is seen on Śivas head in pictures, and from which a sort. of juice exudes. It is the retaining of this exudation which makes one immortal.

गोमांसं भक्षयेन्नित्यं पिबेदमरवारुणीम्।
कुलीनं तमहं मन्ये इतरे कुलघातकाः।। ४६।।

46. Those who eat the flesh of the cow and drink the immortal liquor daily, are regarded by me men of noble family. Others are but a disgrace to their families.

Note— कृतार्थौ पितरौ तेन धन्यो देशः कुलं च तत्।
जायते योगवान्यत्र दत्तमक्षय्यतां व्रजेत्।।
दृष्टः संभाषितः स्पृष्टः पुंप्रकृत्या विवेकवान्।
भवकोटि शतापातं पुनाति वृजिनं नृणाम्।।

ब्रह्मवैवर्त्ते

Translation : Fortunate are the parents and blessed is the country and the family where a Yogī is born. Anything given to such a Yogī, becomes immortal. One, who discriminates between Puruṣa and Prakṛti, purges the sins of a million incarnations, by seeing, speaking, and touching such men (*i.e.,* Yogī).

गृहस्थानां सहस्रेण वानप्रस्थशतेनच।
ब्रह्मचारिसहस्रेण योगाभ्यासी विशिष्यते।

ब्रह्मांडे

A Yogī far exceeds a thousand householders, a hundred vānaprasthas, and a thousand Brahmacārīs.

राजयोगस्य महात्म्यं कोविजानातितत्वतः।
तज्ज्ञानीवसतेयत्र सदेशोपुण्यभाजनम्।।
दर्शनादर्चनादस्य त्रिसप्तकुल संयुताः
अज्ञामुक्तिपदंयान्ति किं पुनस्तत्परायणाः।।
अंतर्योगं बहिर्योगं यो जानातिविशेषतः
त्वया मयाप्यसौवंद्यः शेषैर्वंद्यस्तु कापुनः।।

राजयोग, कूर्म्मपुराणे

एक कालं द्विकालं वा त्रिकालं नित्यमेववा।
ये युञ्जतेमहायोगं विज्ञे यास्ते महेश्वराः।।

Who can know the reality of the Rāja Yoga? That country is very sacred where resides a man who knows it. By seeing and honouring him, generations of ignorant men get mokṣa, what to speak of those who are actually engaged in it. He who knows internal and external yoga, deserves adoration from you and me, what if he is adored by the rest of mankind.

Those who engage in the great yoga, once, twice or thrice daily, are to be known as masters of great wealth (Maheśvaras) or Lords.

गोशब्देनोदिता जिह्वा तत्प्रवेशो हि तालुनि।
गोमांसभक्षणं तत्तु महापातकनाशनम्॥ ४७॥

47. The word गो means tongue; eating it is thrusting it in the gullet which destroys great sins.

जिह्वाप्रवेशसंभूतवह्निनोत्पादितः खलु।
चंद्रात्स्रवति यः सारः स स्यादमरवारुणी॥ ४८॥

48. Immortal liquor is the nectar exuding from the moon (Candra situated on the left side of the space between the eyebrows). It is produced by the fire which is generated by thrusting the tongue.

चुंबंती यदि लंबिकाग्रमनिशं जिह्वारसस्यंदिनी
साक्षारा कटुकाम्लदुग्धसदृशी मध्वाज्यतुल्या तथा।
व्याधीनां हरणं जरांतकरणं शस्त्रागमोदीरणं
तस्य स्यादमरत्वमष्टगुणितं सिद्धांगनाकर्षणम्॥ ४९॥

49. If the tongue can touch with its end the hole from which falls the rasa (juice) which is saltish, bitter, sour, milky and similar to ghee and honey, one can drive away disease, destroy old age, can evade an attack of arms, become immortal in eight ways and can attract fairies.

मूर्ध्नः षोडशपत्रपद्मगलितं प्राणादवाप्तं
हठादूर्ध्वास्यो रसनां नियम्य विवरे शक्तिं परां चिंतयन्।
उत्कल्लोलकलाजलं च विमलं धारामयं यः
पिबेन्निर्व्याधिः स मृणालकोमलवपुर्योगी चिरं जीवति॥५०॥

50. He who drinks the clear stream of liquor of the moon (soma) falling from the brain to the sixteen-petalled lotus (in the heart), obtained by means of Prāṇa, by applying the tongue to the hole of the pendant in the palate, and by meditating on the great power (Kuṇḍalinī), becomes free from disease and tender in body, like the stalk of a lotus, and the Yogī lives a very long life.

यत्प्रालेयं प्रहितसुषिरं मेरुमूर्धा तरस्थं
तस्मिंस्तत्वं प्रवदति सुधीस्तन्मुखं निम्नगानाम्।
चंद्रात्सारः स्रवति वपुषस्तेन मृत्युर्नराणां
तद्बध्नीयात्सुकरणामथो नान्यथा कार्यसिद्धिः॥ ५१॥

51. On the top of the Meru (vertebral column), concealed in a hole, is the Somarasa (nectar of Candra); the wise, whose intellect is not overpowered by Raja and Tama gaṇa, but in whom Satva guṇa is predominant, say there is the (universal spirit) ātma in it. It is the source of the down-going Iḍā, Piṅgalā and Suṣumnā Nāḍīs, which are the Ganges, the Yamunā and the Sarasvatī. From that Candra is shed the essence of the body which causes death of men. It should, therefore, be stopped from shedding. This (Khecarī Mudrā) is a very good instrument for this purpose. There is no other means of achieving this end.

सुषिरं ज्ञानजनकं पंचस्रोतः समन्वितम्।
तिष्ठते खेचरी मुद्रा तस्मिन् शून्ये निरंजने॥ ५२॥

52. This hole is the generator of knowledge and is the source of the five streams (Iḍā, Piṅgalā, etc.). In that colorless vacuum, Khecarī Mudrā should be established.

एकं सृष्टिमयं बीजमेका मुद्रा च खेचरी।
एको देवो निरालंब एकाधस्था मनोन्मनी॥ ५३॥

53. There is only one seed germinating the whole universe from it; and there is only one Mudrā, called Khecarī. There is only one deva (god) without any one's support, and there is one condition called Manonmanī.

अथोड्डीयानबंधः

बद्धो येन सुषुम्नायां प्राणास्तूड्डीयते यतः।
तस्मादुड्डीयनाख्योऽयं योगिभिः समुदाहृतः॥ ५४॥

The Uḍḍīyāna Bandha

54. Uḍḍīyāna is so called, by the Yogīs because by its practice the Prāṇa (Vāyu,) flies (flows) in the Suṣumnā.

उड्डीनं कुरुते यस्मादविश्रांतं महाखगः।
उड्डीयानं तदेव स्यात्तत्र बंधोऽभिधीयते॥ ५५॥

55. Uḍḍīyāna is so called, because the great bird, Prāṇa, tied to it, flies without being fatigued. It is explained below.

उदरे पश्चिमं तानं नाभेरूर्ध्वंच कारयेत्।
उड्डीयानो ह्यसौ बंधो मृत्युमातंगकेसरी॥ ५६॥

56. The belly above the navel is pressed backwards towards the spine. This Uḍḍīyāna Bandha is like a lion for the elephant of death.

उड्डियानं तु सहजं गुरुणा कथितं सदा।
अभ्यसेत्सततं यस्तु वृद्धोऽपि तरुणायते॥ ५७॥

57. Uḍḍīyāna is always very easy, when learnt from a guru. The practiser of this, if old, becomes young again.

नाभेरूर्ध्वमधश्चापि तानं कुर्यात्प्रयत्नतः।
षण्मासमभ्यसेन्मृत्युं जयत्येव न संशयः॥ ५८॥

58. The portions above and below the navel, should be drawn backwards towards the spine. By practising this for six months one can undoubtedly conquer death.

सर्वेषामेव बंधानामुत्तमो ह्युड्डियानकः।
उड्डियाने दृढे बंधे मुक्तिः स्वाभाविकी भवेत्॥ ५९॥

59. Of all the Bandhas, Uḍḍīyāna is the best; for by binding it firmly liberation comes spontaneously.

अथ मूलबंधः

पार्ष्णिभागेन संपीड्य योनिमाकुंचयेद्गुदम्।
अपानमूर्ध्वमाकृष्य मूलबंधोऽभिधीयते॥ ६०॥

The Mūla Bandha

60. Pressing Yoni (perineum) with the heel, contract up the anus. By drawing the Apāna thus, Mūla Bandha is made.

अधोगतिमपानं वा ऊर्ध्वगं कुरुते बलात्।
आकुंचनेन तं प्राहुर्मूलबंधं हि योगिनः॥ ६१॥

61. The Apāna, naturally inclining downward, is made to go up by force. This Mūla Bandha is spoken of by Yogīs as done by contracting the anus.

गुदं पार्ष्ण्या तु संपीड्य वायुमाकुंचयेद् बलात्।
वारंवारं यथा चोर्ध्वं समायाति समीरणः॥ ६२॥

62. Pressing the heel well against the anus, draw up the air by force, again and again till it (air) goes up.

प्राणापानौ नादबिंदू मूलबंधेन चैकताम्।
गत्वा योगस्य संसिद्धिं गच्छतो नात्र संशयः॥ ६३॥

63. Prāṇa, Apāna, Nāda and Bindu uniting into one in this way, give success in Yoga, undoubtedly.

अपानप्राणयोरैक्यं क्षयो मूत्रपुरीषयोः।
युवा भवति वृद्धोऽपि सततं मूलबंधनात्॥ ६४॥

64. By the purification of Prāṇa, and Apāna, urine and excrements decrease. Even an old man becomes young by constantly practising Mūla Bandha.

अपाने ऊर्ध्वगे जाते प्रयाते वह्नि मंडलम्।
तदाऽनलशिखा दीर्घा जायते वायुनाऽहता॥ ६५॥

65. Going up, the Apāna enters the zone of fire, *i.e.*, the stomach. The flame of fire struck by the air is thereby lengthened.

Note— देहमध्ये शिखिस्थानं तप्तजाम्बूनदप्रभम्।
त्रिकोणांत मनुष्याणां चातुरस्रं चतुष्पदाम्॥
मण्डलं तु पतंगानां सत्यमेतद्ब्रवीमि ते।
तन्मध्येतु शिखातन्वी सदा तिष्ठति पावके॥

याज्ञवल्क्ये

In the centre of the body is the seat of fire, like heated gold.
In men it is triangular, in quadrupeds square, in birds circular.
There is a long thin flame in this fire.
It is gastric fire.

ततो यातो वह्न्यपानौ प्राणमुष्णस्वरूपकम्।
तेनात्यंतप्रदीप्तस्तु ज्वलनो देहजस्तथा॥ ६६॥

66. These, fire and Apāna, go to the naturally hot Prāṇa, which, becoming inflamed thereby, causes burning sensation in the body.

तेन कुंडलिनी सुप्ता संतप्ता संप्रबुध्यते।
दंडाहता भुजंगीव निश्वस्य ऋजुतां व्रजेत्॥ ६७॥

67. The Kuṇḍalinī, which has been sleeping all this time, becomes well heated by this means and awakens well. It becomes straight like a serpent, struck dead with a stick.

बिलं प्रविष्टेव ततो ब्रह्मनाड्यंतरं व्रजेत्।
तस्मान्नित्यं मूलबंधः कर्तव्यो योगिभिः सदा॥ ६८॥

68. It enters the Brahma Nāḍī, just as a serpent enters its hole. Therefore, the Yogī should always practise this Mūla Bandha.

अथ जालंधरबंधः

कंठमाकुंच्य हृदये स्थापयेच्चिबुकं दृढम्।
बंधो जालंधराख्योऽयं जरामृत्युविनाशकः॥ ६९॥

The Jālandhara Bandha

69. Contract the throat and press the chin firmly

against the chest. This is called Jālandhara Bandha, which destroys old age and death.

बध्नाति हि शिराजालमधोगामि नभोजलम्।
ततो जालंधरो बंधः कंठदुःखौघनाशनः।। ७०।।

70. It stops the opening (hole) of the group of the Nāḍīs, through which the juice from the sky (from the Soma or Candra in the brain) falls down. It is, therefore, called the Jālandhara Bandha—the destroyer of a host of diseases of the throat.

जालंधरे कृते बंधे कंठसंकोचलक्षणे।
न पीयूषं पतत्यग्नौ न च वायुः प्रकुप्यति।। ७१।।

71. In Jālandhara Bandha, the indications of a perfect contraction of throat are, that the nectar does not fall into the fire (the Sūrya situated in the navel), and the air is not disturbed.

कंठसंकोचनेनैव द्वे नाड्यौ स्तंभयेद्दृढम्।
मध्यचक्रमिदं ज्ञेयं षोडशाधारबंधनम्।। ७२।।

72. The two Nāḍīs should be stopped firmly by contracting the throat. This is called the middle circuit or centre (Madhya Cakra), and it stops the 16 ādhāras (*i.e.*, vital parts).

Note— अंगुष्ठ गुल्फ जानूरु सीवनी लिंगनाभयः।
हृद्ग्रीवा कंठदेशश्च लंबिका नासिका तथा।।
भ्रूमध्यं च ललाटं च मूर्धंच ब्रह्मरंध्रकम्।
एतेहि षोडशाधाराः कथिता योगिपुंगवैः।।

The sixteen vital parts mentioned by renowned Yogīs are the (1) thumbs, (2) ankles, (8) knees, (4) thighs, (5) the prepuce, (6) organs of generation, (7) the navel, (8) the heart, (9) the neck, (10) the throat, (11) the palate, (12) the nose, (13) the middle of the eyebrows, (14) the forehead, (15) the head and (16) the Brahma randhra.

मूलस्थानं समाकुंच्य उड्डीयानं तु करायेत्।
इडां च पिंगलां बध्वा वाहयेत्पश्चिमे पथि।। ७३।।

73. By drawing up the mūlasthāna (anus,) Uḍḍīyāna Bandha should be performed. The flow of the air should be directed to the Suṣumnā, by closing the Iḍā and the Piṅgalā.

अनेनैव विधानेन प्रयाति पावनो लयम्।
ततो न जायते मृत्युर्जरारोगादिकं तथा।। ७४।।

74. The Prāṇa becomes calm and latent by this means, aud thus there is no death, old age, disease, etc.

बंधत्रयमिदं श्रेष्ठं महासिद्धैश्च सेवितम्।
सर्वेषां हठतंत्राणां साधनं योगिनो विदुः।। ७५।।

75. These three Bandhas are the best of all and have been practised by the masters. Of all the means of success in the Haṭha Yoga, they are known to the Yogīs as the chief ones.

यत्किंचित्स्रवते चंद्रादमृतं दिव्यरूपिणः।
तत्सर्वं ग्रसते सूर्यस्तेन पिंडो जरायुतः।। ७६।।

76. The whole of the nectar, possessing divine qualities, which exudes from the Soma (Candra) is devoured by the Sūrya; and, owing to this, the body becomes old.

तत्रास्ति करणं दिव्यं सूर्यस्य मुखवंचनम्।
गुरूपदेशतो ज्ञेयं न तु शास्त्रार्थकोटिभिः।। ७७।।

77. To remedy this, the opening of the Sūrya is avoided by excellent means. It is to be learnt best by instructions from a guru; but not by even a million discussions.

अथ विपरीतकरणी

ऊर्ध्वं नाभेरधस्तालोरूर्ध्वं भानुरधः शशी।
करणी विपरीताख्या गुरुवाक्येन लभ्यते।। ७८।।

The Viparīta Karaṇī

78. Above the navel and below the palate respectively, are the Sūrya and the Candra. The exercise, called the Viparīta Karaṇī, is learnt from the guru's instructions.

नित्यमभ्यासयुक्तस्य जठराग्निविवर्धिनी।
आहारो बहुलस्तस्य संपाद्यः साधकस्य च।
अल्पाहारो यदि भवेदग्निर्दहति तत्क्षणात्॥ ७९॥

79. This exercise increases the appetite; and, therefore, one who practises it, should obtain a good supply of food. If the food be scanty, it will burn him at once.

अधःशिराश्चोर्ध्वपादः क्षणं स्यात्प्रथमे दिने।
क्षणाच्च किंचिदधिकमभ्यसेच्च दिने दिने॥ ८०॥

80. Place the head on the ground and the feet up into the sky, for a second only the first day, and increase this time daily.

वलितं पलितं चैव षण्मासोर्ध्वं न दृश्यते।
याममत्रं तु यो नित्यमभ्यसेत्स तु कालजित्॥ ८१॥

81. After six months, the wrinkles and grey hair are not seen. He who practises it daily, even for two hours, conquers death.

अथ वज्रोली

स्वेच्छया वर्तमानोऽपि योगोक्तैर्नियमैर्विना।
वज्रोलीं यो विजानाति स योगी सिद्धिभाजनम्॥ ८२॥

TheeVajrolī

82. Even if one who lives a wayward life, without observing any rules of Yoga, but performs Vajrolī, deserves success and is a Yogī.

तत्रवस्तुद्वयं वक्ष्ये दुर्लभं यस्य कस्य चित्!
क्षीरं चैकं द्वितीयं तु नारी च वशवर्तिनी॥ ८३॥

83. Two things are necessary for this, and these

are difficult to get for the ordinary people—(1) milk and (2) a woman behaving, as desired.

मेहनेन शनैः सम्यगूर्ध्वाकुंचनमभ्यसेत्।
पुरुषोऽप्यथवा नारी वज्रोलीसिद्धिमाप्नुयात्॥ ८४॥

84. By practising to draw in the *bindu,* discharged during cohabitation, whether one be a man or a woman, one obtains success in the practice of Vajrolī.

यत्नतः शस्तनालेन फूत्कारं वज्रकंदरे।
शनैः शनैः प्रकुर्वीत वायुसंचारकारणात्॥ ८५॥

85. By means of a pipe, one should blow air slowly into the passage in the male organ.

नारीभगे पतद्बिंदुमभ्यासेनोर्ध्वमाहरेत्।
चलितं च निजं बिंदुमूर्ध्वमाकृष्य रक्षयेत्॥ ८६॥

86. By practice, the discharged *bindu* is drawn out. One can draw back and preserve one's own discharged *bindu.*

एवं संरक्षयेद् बिंदुं मृत्युं जयति योगवित्।
मरणं बिंदुपातेन जीवनं बिंदुधारणात्॥ ८७॥

87. The Yogī who can protect his *bindu* thus, overcomes death; because death comes by discharging *bindu,* and life is prolonged by its preservation.

सुगंधो योगिनो देहे जायते बिंदुधारणात्।
यावद् बिंदुः स्थिरो देहे तावत्कालभयं कुतः॥ ८८॥

88. By preserving *bindu,* the body of the Yogī emits a pleasing smell. There is no fear of death, so long as the *bindu* is well-established in the body.

चित्तायतं नृणां शुक्रं शुक्रायत्तं च जीवितम्।
तस्माच्छुक्रं मनश्चैव रक्षणीयं प्रयत्नतः॥ ८९॥

89. The *bindu* of men is under the control of the mind, and life is dependent on the *bindu.* Hence, mind and *bindu* should be protected by all means.

अथ सहजोलि

सहजोलिचामरोलिर्वज्रोल्या भेद एकतः।
जलेषु भस्म निक्षिप्य दग्धगोमयसंभवम्॥ ९०॥

The Sahajalī

90. Sahajolī and Amarolī are only the different kinds of Vajrolī. Ashes from burnt up cowdung should be mixed with water.

वज्रोलीमैथुनादूर्ध्वं स्त्रीपुंसोः स्वागंलेपनम्।
आसीनयोः सुखेनैव मुक्तव्यापयोः क्षणात्॥ ९१॥

91. Being free from the exercise of Vajrolī, man and woman should both rub it on their bodies.

सहजोलिरियं प्रोक्ता श्रद्धेया योगिभिः सदा।
अयं शुभकारो योगो भोगयुक्तोऽपि मुक्तिदः॥ ९२॥

92. This is called Sahajolī, and should be relied on by Yogīs. It does good and gives mokṣa.

अयं योगः पुण्यवतां धीरणां तत्वदर्शिनाम्।
निर्मत्सराणां सिध्येत न तु मत्सरशालिनाम्॥ ९३॥

93. This Yoga is achieved by courageous wise men, who are free from sloth, and cannot be accomplished by the slothful.

अथामरोली

पित्तोल्वणात्वात्प्रथमांबुधारां
विहाय निःसारतयांत्यधारा।
निषेव्यते शीतलमध्यधारा
कापालिके खंडमतेऽमरोली॥ ९४॥

The Amarolī

94. In the doctrine of the sect of the Kāpālikas, the Amarolī is the drinking of the mid stream; leaving the 1st, as it is a mixture of too much bile and the last, which is useless.

अमरीं यः पिबेन्नित्यं नस्यं कुर्वन् दिने दिने।
वज्रोलीमभ्यसेत्सम्यगमरोलीति कथ्यते॥ ८५॥

95. He who drinks Amarī, snuffs it daily, and practices Vajrolī, is called practising Amarolī.

अभ्यासान्निःसृता चांद्रीं विभूत्या सह मिश्रयेत्।
धारयेदुत्तमांगेषु दिव्यदृष्टिः प्रजायते॥ ९६॥

96. The *bindu* discharged in the practice of Vajrolī should be mixed with ashes, and the rubbing it on the best parts of the body gives divine sight.

अथ शक्तिचालनं

कुटिलांगी कुंडलिनी भुजंगी शक्तिरीश्वरी।
कुंडल्यरुंधती चैते शब्दाः पर्यायवाचकाः॥ ९७॥

The Śakti cālana

97. Kuṭilāṅgī (crooked-bodied), Kuṇḍalinī, Bhujaṅgī (a she-serpent) Śakti, Īśvarī, Kuṇḍalī, Arundhatī,—all these words are synonymous.

उद्घाटयेत्कपाटं तु यथा कुंचिकया हठात्।
कुंडलिन्या तथा योगी मोक्षद्वारं विभेदयेत्॥ ९८॥

98. As a door is opened with a key, so the Yogī opens the door of mukti by opening Kuṇḍalinī by means of Haṭha yoga.

येन मार्गेण गंतव्यं ब्रह्मस्थानं निरामयम्।
मुखेनाच्छाद्य तद्वारं प्रसुप्ता परमेश्वरी॥ ९९॥

99. The Parameśvarī (Kuṇḍalinī) sleeps, covering the hole of the passage by which one can go to the seat of Brahma which is free from pains.

कंदोर्ध्वं कुंडली शक्तिः सुप्ता मोक्षाय योगिनाम्।
बंधनाय च मूढानां यस्तां वेत्ति स योगवित्॥ १००॥

100. Kuṇḍalī Śakti sleeps on the bulb, for the purpose of giving mokṣa to Yogīs and bondage to the ignorant. He who knows it, knows Yoga.

कुंडली कुटिलाकारा सर्पवत्परिकीर्तिता।
सा शक्तिश्चालिता येन स मुक्तो नात्र संशयः॥ १०१॥

101. Kuṇḍalī is of a bent shape, and has been described to be like a serpent. He who has moved that Śakti is no doubt Mukta (released from bondage).

गंगायमुनयोर्मध्ये बालरंडा तपस्विनी।
बलात्कारेण गृह्णीयात्तद्विष्णोः परमं पदम्॥ १०२॥

102. Youngster Tapasvinī (a she-ascetic), lying between the Ganges and the Yumunā, (Iḍā and Piṅgalā) should be caught hold of by force, to get the highest position.

इडा भगवती गंगा पिंगला यमुना नदी।
इडापिंगलयोर्मध्ये बालरंडा च कुंडली॥ १०३॥

103. Iḍā is called goddess Ganges, Piṅgalā goddess Yamunā. In the middle of the Iḍā and the Piṅgalā is the infant widow, Kuṇḍalī.

पुच्छे प्रगृह्य भुजगीं सुप्तामुंद्बोधयेच्च ताम्।
निद्रां विहाय सा शक्तिरूर्ध्वमुत्तिष्ठते हठात्॥ १०४॥

104. This sleeping she-serpent should be awakened by catching hold of her tail. By the force of Haṭha, the Śakti leaves her sleep, and starts upwards.

अवस्थिता चैव फणावती
सा प्रातश्च सायं प्रहरार्धमात्रम्।
प्रपूर्य सूर्यात्परिधानयुक्त्या
प्रगृह्य नित्यं परिचालनीया॥ १०५॥

105. This she-serpent is situated in Mūlādhāra. She should be caught and moved daily, morning and evening, for ½ a prahar (1½hours), by filling with air through Piṅgalā by the Paridhāna method.

ऊर्ध्वं वितस्तिमात्रं तु विस्तारं चतुरंगुलम्।
मृदुलं धवलं प्रोक्तं वेष्टितांबरलक्षणम्॥ १०६॥

106. The bulb is above the anus, a vitasti (12 aṅgulas) long, and measures 4 aṅgulas (3 inches) in extent and is soft and white, and appears as if a folded cloth.

सति वज्रासने पादौ कराभ्यां धारयेद्दृढम्।
गुल्फदेशसमीपे च कंदं तत्र प्रपीडयेत्॥ १०७॥

107. Keeping the feet in Vajra-āsana (Padma-āsana), hold them firmly with the hands. The position of the bulb then will be near the ankle joint, where it should be pressed.

वज्रासने स्थितो योगी चालयित्वा च कुंडलीम्।
कुर्यादनंतरं भस्त्रां कुंडलीमाशु बोधयेत्॥ १०८॥

108. The Yogī, sitting with Vajra-āsana and having moved Kuṇḍalī, should perfom Bhastrikā to awaken the Kuṇḍalī soon.

भानोराकुंचनं कुर्यात्कुंडलीं चालयेत्ततः।
मृत्युवक्त्रगतस्यापि तस्य मृत्युभयं कुतः॥ १०९॥

109. Bhānu (Sūrya, near the navel) should be contracted (by contracting the navel) which will move the Kuṇḍalī. There is no fear for him who does so, even if he has entered the month of death.

मुहूर्तद्वयपर्यंतं निर्भयं चालनादसौ।
ऊर्ध्वमाकृष्यते किंचित्सुषुम्नायां समुद्गता॥ ११०॥

110. By moving this, for two muhūrtas, it is drawn up a little by entering the Suṣumnā (spinal column).

तेन कुंडलिनी तस्याः सुषुम्नायां मुखं ध्रुवम्।
जहाति तस्मात्प्राणोऽयं सुषुम्नां व्रजति स्वतः॥ १११॥

111. By this Kuṇḍalinī leaves the entrance of the Suṣumnā at once, and the Prāṇa enters it of itself.

तस्मात्संचालयेन्नित्यं सुखसुप्तामरुंधतीम्।
तस्याः संचालनेनैव योगी रोगैः प्रमुच्यते॥ ११२॥

112. Therefore, this comfortably sleeping Arundhatī should always be moved; for by so doing the

Yogī gets rid of diseases.

येन संचालिता शक्तिः च योगी सिद्धिभाजनम्।
किमत्र बहुनोक्तेन कालं जयति लीलया॥ ११३॥

113. The Yogī, who has been able to move the Śakti deserves success. It is useless to say more, suffice it to say that he conquers death playfully.

ब्रह्मचर्यरतस्यैव नित्यं हितमिताशिनः।
मंडलाद्दृश्यते सिद्धिः कुंडल्यभ्यासयोगिनः॥ ११४॥

114. The Yogī observing Brahmacarya (continence) and always eating sparingly, gets success within 40 days by practice with the Kuṇḍalinī.

कुंडलीं चालयित्वा तु भस्त्रां कुर्याद्विशेषतः।
एवमभ्यसतो नित्यं यमिनो यमभीः कुतः॥ ११५॥

115. After moving the Kuṇḍalī, plenty of Bhastrā should be performed. By such practice, he has no fear from the god of death.

द्वासप्ततिसहस्राणां नाडीनां मलशोधने।
कुतः प्रक्षालनोपायः कुंडल्यभ्यसनादृते॥ ११६॥

116. There is no other way, but the practice of the Kuṇḍalī, for washing away the impurities of 72,000 Nāḍīs.

इयं तु मध्यमा नाडी दृढाभ्यासेन योगिनाम्।
आसनप्राणसंयाममुद्राभिः सरला भवेत्॥ ११७॥

117. This middle Nāḍī becomes straight by steady practice of postures; Prāṇāyāma and Mudrās of Yogīs.

अभ्यासे तु विनिद्राणां मनो धृत्वा समाधिना।
रुद्राणी वा यदा मुद्रा भद्रां सिद्धिं प्रयच्छति॥ ११८॥

118. Those whose sleep has decreased by practice and mind has become calm by samādhi, get beneficial accomplishments by Śāmbhavī and other Mudrās.

राजयोगं विना पृथ्वी राजयोगं विना निशा।
राजयोगं विना मुद्रा विचित्रापि न शोभते॥ ११९॥

119. Without Rāja Yoga, this earth, the night, and the Mudrās, be they howsoever wonderful, do not appear beautiful.

Note—Rāja Yoga = āsana. Earth = steadiness, calmness. Night = Kumbhaka; cessations of the activity of the Prāṇa, just as King's officials cease moving at night. Hence night means absence of motion, *i.e.*, Kumbhaka.

मारुतस्य विधिं सर्वं मनोयुक्तं समभ्यसेत्।
इतरत्र न कर्तव्या मनोवृत्तिर्मनीषिणा॥ १२०॥

120. All the practices relating to the air should be performed with concentrated mind. A wise man should not allow his mind to wander away.

इति मुद्रा दश प्रोक्ता आदिनाथेन शंभुना।
एकैका तासु यमिनां महासिद्धिप्रदायिनी॥ १२१॥

121. These are the Mudrās, as explained by Ādinātha (Śiva). Every one of them is the giver of great accomplishments to the practiser.

उपेदशं हि मुद्राणां यो दत्ते सांप्रदायिकम्।
स एव श्रीगुरुः स्वामी साक्षादीश्वर एव सः॥ १२२॥

122. He is really the *guru* and to be considered as Īśvara in human form who teaches the Mudrās as handed down from guru to guru.

तस्य वाक्यपरो भूत्वा मुद्राभ्यासे समाहितः।
अणिमादिगुणैः सार्धं लभते कालवंचनम्॥ १२३॥

123. Engaging in practice, by putting faith in his words, one gets the Siddhis of Aṇimā, etc., as also evades death.

इति हठप्रदीपिकायां तृतीयोपदेशः॥ ३॥

End of chapter III, on the Exposition of the Mudrās.

Chapter IV

चतुर्थोपदेशः

On Samādhi

नमः शिवाय गुरवेनादबिंदुकलात्मने।
निरंजनपदं याति नित्यं यत्र परायणः॥ १॥

1. Salutation to the Guru, the dispenser of happiness to all, appearing as Nāda, Bindū and Kalā. One who is devoted to Him, obtains the highest bliss.

अथेदानीं प्रवक्ष्यामि समाधिक्रममुत्तमम्।
मृत्युघ्नं च सुखोपायं ब्रह्मानंदकरं परम्॥ २॥

2. Now I will describe a regular method of attaining to Samādhi, which destroys death, is the means for obtaining happiness, and gives the Brahmānanda.

राजयोगसमाधिश्च उन्मनी च मनोन्मनी।
अमरत्वं लयस्तत्वं शून्याशून्यं परं पदम्॥ ३॥
अमनस्कं तथा द्वैतं निरालंबं निरंजनम्।
जीवन्मुक्तिश्च सहजा तुर्या चेत्येकवाचकाः॥ ४॥

3–4. Rāja Yogī, Samādhi, Unmanī, Manonmanī, Amaratva, Laya, Tatva, Śūnya, Aśūnya, Parama Pada, Amanaska, Advaitama, Nirālamba, Nirañjana, Jīvana Mukti, Sahajā, Turyā, are all synonymons.

सलिले सैंधवं यद्वत्साम्यं भजति योगतः।
तथात्ममनसोरैक्यं समाधिरभिधीयते॥ ५॥

5. As salt being dissolved in water becomes one with

it, so when Ātmā and mind become one, it is called Samādhi.

यदा संक्षीयते प्राणो मानसं च प्रलीयते।
तदा समरसत्वं च समाधिरभिधीयते॥ ६॥

6. When the Prāṇa becomes lean (vigourless) and the mind becomes absorbed, then their becoming equal is called Samādhi.

तत्समं च द्वयोरैक्यं जीवात्मपरमात्मनोः।
प्रनष्टसर्वसंकल्पः समाधिः सोऽभिधीयते॥ ७॥

7. This equality and oneness of the self and the ultra self, when all Saṅkalpas lease to exist, is called Samādhi.

राजयोगस्य माहात्म्यं को वा जानाति तत्त्वतः।
ज्ञानं मुक्तिः स्थितिः सिद्धिर्गुरुवाक्येन लभ्यते॥ ८॥

8. Or, who can know the true greatness of the Rāja Yoga. Knowledge, mukti, condition, and Siddhīs can be learnt by instructions alone from, a *guru* alone.

दुर्लभो विषयत्यागो दुर्लभं तत्त्वदर्शनम्।
दुर्लभा सहजावस्था सद्गुरोः करुणां विना॥ ९॥

9. Indifference to worldly enjoyments is very difficult to obtain, and equally difficult is the knowledge of the Realities to obtain. It is very difficult to get the condition of Samādhi, without the favour of a true *guru*.

विविधैरासनैः कुंभैर्विचित्रैः करणैरपि।
प्रबुद्धायां महाशक्तौ प्राणः शून्ये प्रलीयते॥ १०॥

10. By means of various postures and different Kumbhakas, when the great power (Kuṇḍalī) awakens, then the Prāṇa becomes absorbed in Śūnya (Samādhi).

उत्पन्नशक्तिबोधस्य त्यक्तनिःशेषकर्मणः।
योगिनः सहजावस्था स्वयमेव प्रजायते॥ ११॥

11. The Yogī whose śakti has awakened, and who

has renounced all actions, attains to the condition of Samādhi, without any effort.

सुषुम्नावाहिनि प्राणे शून्ये विशति मानसे।
तदा सर्वाणि कर्माणि निर्मूलयति योगवित्॥ १२॥

12. When the Prāṇa flows in the Suṣumnā, and the mind has entered śūnya, then the Yogī is free from the effects of Karmas.

अमराय नमस्तुभ्यं सोऽपिकालस्त्वया जितः।
पतितं वदने यस्य जगदेतच्चराचरम्॥ १३॥

13. O Immortal one (that is, the *yogī* who has attained to the condition of Samādhi), I salute thee! Even death itself, into whose mouth the whole of this movable and immovable world has fallen, has been conquered by thee.

चित्ते समत्वमापन्ने वायौ व्रजति मध्यमे।
तदामरोली वज्रोली सहजोली प्रजायते॥ १४॥

14. Amarolī, Vajrolī and Sahajolī are accomplished when the mind becomes calm and Prāṇa has entered the middle channel.

ज्ञानं कुतो मनसि संभवतीह तावत्
प्राणोऽपिजीवति मनो म्रियते न यावत्।
प्राणो मनो द्वयमिदं विलयं नयेद्यो–
मोक्षं स गच्छति नरो न कथंचिदन्यः॥ १५॥

15. How can it be possible to get knowledge, so long as the Prāṇa is living and the mind has not died? No one else can get mokṣa, except one who can make one's Prāṇa and mind latent.

ज्ञात्वा सुषुम्नासद्भेदं कृत्वा वायुं च मध्यगम्।
स्थित्वा सदैव सुस्थाने ब्रह्मरंध्रे निरोधयेत्॥ १६॥

16. Always living in a good locality and having known the secret of the Suṣumnā, which has a middle course, and making the Vāyu move in it, (the Yogī) should restrain the Vāyu in the Brahma randhra.

सूर्याचंद्रमसौ धत्तः कालं रात्रिंदिवात्मकम्।
भोक्त्री सुषुम्ना कालस्य गुह्यमेतदुदाहृतम्॥ १७॥

17. Time, in the form of night and day, is made by the sun and the moon. That the Suṣumnā. devours this time (death) even, is a great secret.

द्वासप्ततिसहस्राणि नाडीद्वाराणि पंजरे।
सुषुम्ना शांभवी शक्तिः शेषास्त्वेव निरर्थकाः॥ १८॥

18. In this body there are 72,000 openings of Nāḍīs; of these, the Suṣumnā, which has the Śāmbhavī Śakti in it, is the only important one, the rest are useless.

वायुः परिचितो यस्मादग्निना सह कुण्डलीम्।
बोधयित्वा सुषुम्नायां प्रविशेदनिरोधतः॥ १९॥

19. The Vāyu should be made to enter the Suṣumnā without restraint by him who has practised the control of breathing and has awakened the Kuṇḍalī by the (gastric) fire.

सुषुम्ना वाहिनि प्राणे सिद्ध्यत्येव मनोन्मनी।
अन्यथा त्वितराभ्यासाः प्रयासायैव योगिनाम्॥ २०॥

20. The Prāṇa, flowing through the Suṣumnā, brings about the condition of manonmanī; other practices are simply futile for the Yogī.

पवनो बध्यते येन मनस्तेनैव बध्यते।
मनश्च बध्यते येन पवनस्तेन बध्यते॥ २१॥

21. By whom the breathing has been controlled, by him the activities of the mind also have been controllecd and, conversely, by whom the activities of the mind have been controlled, by him the breathing also has been controlled.

हेतुद्वयं तु चित्तस्य वासना च समीरणः।
तयोर्विनष्ट एकस्मिन्तौ द्वावपि विनश्यतः॥ २२॥

22. There are two causes of the activities of the mind:

(1) Vāsanā (desires) and (2) the respiration (the Prāṇa). Of these, the destruction of the one is the destruction of both.

मनो यत्र विलीयेत पवनस्तत्र लीयते।
पवनो लीयते यत्र मनस्तत्र विलीयते॥ २३॥

23. Breathing is lessened when the mind becomes absorbed, and the mind becomes absorbed when the Prāṇa is restrained.

दुग्धांबुवत्संमिलिता वुभौ तौ
तुल्यक्रियौमानस मारुतौहि।
यतो मरुत्तत्रमनःप्रवृत्तिर्यतो
मनस्तत्र मरुत्प्रवत्तिः॥ २४॥

24. Both the mind and the breath are united together, like milk and water; and both of them are equal in their activities. Mind begins its activities where there is the breath, and the Prāṇa begins its activities where there is the mind.

तत्रैकनाशादपरस्य नाश
एकप्रवृत्तेरपरप्रवृत्तिः।
अध्वस्तयोश्चेंद्रियवर्गवृत्तिः-
प्रध्वस्तयोर्मोक्षपदस्य सिद्धिः॥ २५॥

25. By the suspension of the one, therefore, comes the suspension of the other, and by the operations of the one are brought about the operations of the other. When they are present, the Indriyas (the senses) remain engaged in their proper functions, and when they become latent then there is mokṣa.

रसस्य मनसश्चैव चंचलत्वं स्वभावतः।
रसो बद्धो मनो बद्धं किन्न सिद्धयति भूतले॥ २६॥

26. By nature, Mercury and mind are unsteady: there is nothing in the world which cannot be accomplished when these are made steady.

मूर्च्छितोहरते व्याधीन्मृतो जीवयति स्वयम्।

बद्धः खेचरतां धत्ते रसो वायुश्च पार्वति॥ २७॥

27. O Pārvatī! Mercury and breathing, when made steady, destroy diseases and the dead himself comes to life (by their means). By their (proper) control, moving in the air is attained.

मनः स्थैर्ये स्थिरो वायुस्ततो बिंदुः स्थिरो भवेत्।
बिंदुस्थैर्यात्सदा सत्वं पिंडस्थैर्यं प्रजायते॥ २८॥

28. The breathing is calmed when the mind becomes steady and calm; and hence the preservation of *bindu*. The preservation of this latter makes the satva established in the body.

इंद्रियाणां मनो नाथो मनोनाथस्तु मारुतः।
मारुतस्यलयोनाथः सलयो नादमाश्रितः॥ २९॥

29. Mind is the master of the senses, and the breath is the master of the mind. The breath in its turn is subordinate to the laya (absorption), and that laya depends on the nāda.

सोऽयमेवास्तु मोक्षाख्यो मास्तु वापि मतांतरे।
मनः प्राणलये कश्चिदानंदः संप्रवर्तते॥ ३०॥

30. This very laya is what is called mokṣa, or, being a sectarian, you may not call it mokṣa; but when the mind becomes absorbed, a sort of ecstacy is experienc-ed.

प्रनष्टश्वासनिश्वासः प्रध्वस्तविषयग्रहः।
निश्चेष्टो निर्विकारश्च लयो जयति योगिनाम्॥ ३१॥

31. By the suspension of respiration and the annihilation of the enjoyments of the senses, when the mind becomes devoid of all the activities and remains changeless, then the Yogī attains to the Laya Stage.

उच्छिन्नसर्वसंकल्पो निःशेषाशेषचेष्टितः।
स्वावगम्यो लयः कोऽपि जायते वागगोचरः॥ ३२॥

32. When all the thoughts and activities are destroyed, then the Laya Stage is produced, to describe which is beyond the power of speech, being known by self-experience alone.

लयो लय इति प्राहुः कीदृशं लयक्षणम्।
अपुनर्वासनोत्थानाल्लयो विषयविस्मृतिः॥ ३३॥

33. They often speak of Laya, Laya; but what is meant by it?

Laya is simply the forgetting of the objects of senses when the Vāsanās (desires) do not rise into existence again.

अथ शांभवी मुद्रा

वेदशास्त्रपुराणानि सामान्यगणिका इव।
एकैव शांभवी मुद्रा गुप्ता कुलवधूरिव॥ ३४॥

The Śāmbhavī Mudrā

34. The Vedas and the Śāstras are like ordinary public women. Śāmbhavī Mudrā is the one, which is secluded like a respectable lady.

अंतर्लक्ष्यं वहिर्दृष्टिर्निमेषोन्मेषवर्जिता।
एषा सा शांभवी मुद्रा वेदशास्त्रेषु गोपिता॥ ३५॥

35. Aiming at Brahman inwardly, while keeping the sight directed to the external objects, without blinking the eyes, is called the Śāmbhavī Mudrā, hidden in the Vedas and the Śāstras.

अंतर्लक्ष्यविलीनचित्तपवनो योगी यदा वर्तते,
दृष्ट्या निश्चलतारया बहिरधः पश्यन्नपश्यन्नपि।
मुद्रेयं खलु शांभवी भवति सा लब्ध्वा प्रसादाद् गुरोः,
शून्याशून्यविलक्षणं स्फुरति तत्तत्वं परं शांभवम्॥ ३६॥

36. When the Yogī remains inwardly attentive to the Brahman, keeping the mind and the Prāṇa absorbed, and the sight steady, as if seeing everything while in reality seeing nothing outside, below, or above, verily then it is called the Śāmbhavī Mudrā, which is learnt by the favour of a *guru*. Whatever, wonderful, Śūnya or Aśūnya is perceived, is to be regarded as the manifestation of that great Śambhū (Śiva.)

श्रीशांभव्याश्च खेचर्या अवस्थाधामभेदतः।
भवेच्चित्तलयानंदः शून्ये चित्सुखरूपिणि॥ ३७॥

37. The two states, the Śāmbhavī and the Khecarī, are different because of their seats (being the heart and the space between the eyebrows respectively); but both cause happiness, for the mind becomes absorbed in the Citta-sukha-Rūpa-ātman which is void.

अथोन्मनी

तारे ज्योतिषि संयोज्य किंचिदुन्नमयेद् भ्रुवौ।
पूर्वयोगं मनोयुंजन्नुन्मनीकारकः क्षणात्॥ ३८॥

The Unmanī

38. Fix the gaze on the light (seen on the tip of the nose) and raise the eyebrows a little, with the mind contemplating as before (in the Śāmbhavī Mudrā, that is, inwardly thinking of Brahma, but apparently looking outside). This will create the Unmanī avasthā at once.

केचिदागमजाले केचिन्निगमसंकुलैः।
केचित्तर्केण मुह्यंति नैव जानंति तारकम्॥ ३९॥

The Tarka

39. Some are devoted to the Vedas, some to Nigama, while others are enwrapt in Logic, but none knows the value of this mudrā, which enables one to cross the ocean of existence.

अर्धोन्मीलितलोचनः स्थिरमना नासाग्रदत्तेक्षणाः
चद्रार्कावपि लीनतामुपनयन्निस्पंदभावेन यः।
ज्योतिरूपमशेषबीजमखिलं देदीप्यमानं परं
तत्त्वं तत्पदमेति वस्तु परमं वाच्यं किमत्राधिकम्॥ ४०॥

40. With steady calm mind and half closed eyes, fixed on the tip of the nose, stopping the Iḍā and the Piṅgalā without blinking, he who can see the light which is the all, the seed, the entire brilliant, great Tattvam, approaches Him, who is the great object. What is the use of more talk?

दिवा न पूजयेल्लिंगं रात्रौ चैव न पूजयेत्।
सर्वदा पूजयेल्लिंगं दिवारात्रिनिरोधतः॥ ४१॥

41. One should not meditate on the Liṅga (*i.e.*, Ātman) in the day (*i.e.*, while Sūrya or Piṅgalā is working) or at night (when Iḍā is working), but should always contemplate after restraining both.

अथ खेचरी

सव्यदक्षिणानाडिस्थो मध्ये चरति मारुतः।
तिष्ठते खेचरी मुद्रा तस्मिन् स्थानेन संशयः॥ ४२॥

The Khecarī

42. When the air has ceased to move in the right and the left nostrils, and has begun to flow in the middle path, then the Khecarī Mudrā can be accomplished there. There is no doubt of this.

इडापिंगलयोर्मध्ये शून्यं चैवानिलं ग्रसेत्।
तिष्ठते खेचरी मुद्रा तत्र सत्यं पुनः पुनः॥ ४३॥

43. If the Prāṇa can be drawn into the Śūnya (Suṣumnā), which is between the Iḍā and the Piṅgalā, and made motionless there, then the Khecarī Mudrā can truly become steady there.

सूर्याचंद्रमसोर्मध्ये निरालबांतरं पुनः।
संस्थिता व्योमचक्रे या सा मुद्रा नाम खेचरी॥ ४४॥

44. That Mudrā is called Khecarī which is per-formed in the supportless space between the Sūrya and the Candra (the Iḍā and the Piṅgalā) and called the Vyoma Cakra.

सोमाद्यत्रोदिता धारा साक्षात्सा शिववल्लभा।
पूरयेदतुलां दिव्यां सुषुम्नां पश्चिमे मुखे॥ ४५॥

45. The Khecarī which causes the stream to flow from

the Candra (Soma) is beloved of Śiva. The incomparable divine Suṣumnā should be closed by the tongue drawn back.

पुरस्ताच्चैव पूर्येत निश्चिता खेचरी भवेत्।
अभ्यस्ता खेचरी मुद्राप्युन्मनी संप्रजाते॥ ४६॥

46. It can be closed from the front also (by stopping the movements of the Prāṇa), and then surely it becomes the Khecarī. By practice, this Khecarī leads to Unmanī.

भ्रुवोर्मध्ये शिवस्थानं मनस्तत्र विलीयते।
ज्ञातव्यं तत्पदं तुर्यं तत्र कालो न विद्यते॥ ४७॥

47. The seat of Śiva is between the eyebrows, and the mind becomes absorbed there. This condition (in which the mind is thus absorbed) is known as Tūrya, and death has no access there.

अभ्यसेत्खेचरीं तावद्यावस्याद्योगनिद्रितः।
संप्राप्तयोगनिद्रस्य कालो नास्ति कदाचन॥ ४८॥

48. The Khecarī should be practised till there is Yoga-nidrā (Samādhi). One who has induced Yoga-nidrā, cannot fall a victim to death.

निरालंबं मनः कृत्वा न किंचिदपि चिंतयेत्।
सबाह्याभ्यंतरे व्योम्नि घटवत्तिष्ठति ध्रुवम्॥ ४९॥

49. Freeing the mind from all thoughts and thinking of nothing, one should sit firmly like a pot in the space (surrounded and filled with the ether).

बाह्यवायुर्यथा लीनस्तथा मध्ये न संशयः।
स्वस्थाने स्थिरतामेति पवनो मनसा सह॥ ५०॥

50. As the air, in and out of the body, remains unmoved, so the breath with mind becomes steady in its place (*i.e.*, in Brahma randhra).

एवमभ्यसमानस्य वायुमार्गे दिवानिशम्।
अभ्यासाज्जीर्यते वायुर्मनस्तत्रैव लीयये॥ ५१॥

51. By thus practising, night and day, the breathing is brought under control, and, as the practice in-creases, the mind becomes calm and steady.

अमृतैः प्लावयेद्देहमापादतलमस्तकम्।
सिद्ध्यत्येव महाकायो महाबलपराक्रमः॥ ५२॥
इति खेचरी

52. By rubbing the body over with Amṛta (exuding from the moon), from head to foot, one gets Mahākāyā, *i.e.,* great strength and energy.

End of the Khecarī

शक्तिमध्ये मनः कृत्वा शक्तिं मानसमध्यगाम्।
मनसा मन आलोक्य धारयेत्परमं पदम्॥ ५३॥

53. Placing the mind into the Kuṇḍalinī, and getting the latter into the mind, by looking upon the Buddhi (intellect) with mind (reflexively), the Param Pada (Brahma) should be obtained.

खमध्ये कुरु चात्मानमात्ममध्ये च खं कुरु।
सर्वं च खमयं कृत्वा न किंचिदपि चिंतयेत्॥ ५४॥

54. Keep the ātmā inside the Kha (Brahma) and place Brahma inside your ātmā. Having made everything pervaded with Kha (Brahma), think of nothing else.

अंतः शून्यो बहिः शून्यः शून्यः कुंभ इवांबरे।
अंतः पूर्णो बहिः पूर्णाः कुंभ इवार्णवे॥ ५५॥

55. One should become void in and void out, and void like a pot in the space. Full in and full outside, like a jar in the ocean.

बाह्यचिंता न कर्तव्या तथैवांतरचिंतनम्।
सर्वचिंतां परित्यज्य न किंचिदपि चिंतयेत्॥ ५६॥

56. He should be neither of his inside nor of outside world; and, leaving all thoughts, he should think of nothing.

संकल्पमात्रकलनैव जागत्समग्रं
संकल्पमात्रकलनैव मनोविलासः॥
संकल्पमात्रमतिमुत्सृज निर्विकल्प
माश्रित्य निश्चयमवाप्नुहिराम शांतिम्॥ ५७॥

57. The whole of this world and all the schemes of the mind are but the creations of thought. Discarding these thoughts and taking leave of all conjectures, O Rāma! obtain peace.

कर्पूरमनले यद्वत्सैंधवं सलिले तथा।
तथा संधीयमानं च मनस्तत्त्वे विलीयते॥ ५८॥

58. As camphor disappears in fire, and rock salt in water, so the mind united with the ātmā loses its identity.

ज्ञेयं सर्वं प्रतीतं च ज्ञानं च मन उच्यते।
ज्ञानं ज्ञेयं समं नष्टं नान्यः पंथा द्वितीयकः॥ ५९॥

59. When the knowable, and the knowledge, are both destroyed equally, then there is no second way (*i.e.*, Duality is destroyed).

मनोदृश्यमिदं सर्वं यत्किंचित्सचराचरम्।
मनसो ह्युन्मनीभावद्द्वैतं नैवोपलभ्यते॥ ६०॥

60. All this movable and immovable world is mind. When the mind has attained to the unmanī avasthā, there is no dvaita (from the absence of the working of the mind).

ज्ञेयवस्तु परित्यागाद्विलयं याति मानसम्।
मनसो विलये जाते कैवल्यमवशिष्यते॥ ६१॥

61. Mind disappears by removing the knowable, and, on its disappearance, ātmā only remains behind.

एवं नानाविधोपायाः सम्यक् स्वानुभवान्विताः।
समाधिमार्गाः कथिताः पूर्वाचार्यैर्महात्मभिः॥ ६२॥

62. The high-souled Ācāryas (Teachers) of yore gained experience in the various methods of Samādhi themselves, and then they preached them to others.

सुषुम्नायै कुंडलिन्यै सुधायै चंद्रजन्मने।
मनोन्मन्यै नमस्तुभ्यं महाशक्त्यै चिदात्मने॥ ६३॥

63. Salutations to Thee, O Suṣumnā, to Thee O Kuṇḍalinī, to Thee O Sudhā, born of Candra, to Thee O Manonmanī! to Thee O great power, energy and the intelligent spirit.

अशक्यतत्त्वबोधानां मूढानामपि संमतम्।
प्रोक्तं गोरक्षनाथेन नादोपासनमुच्यते॥ ६४॥

64. I will describe now the practice of anāhata nāda, as propounded by Gorakṣa Nātha, for the benefit of those who are unable to understand the principles of knowlerlge—a method, which is liked by the ignorant also.

श्रीआदिनाथेन सपादकोटिलयप्रकाराः किथता जयंति।
नादानुसंधानकमेकमेव मन्यामहे मुख्यतमं लयानाम्॥
६५॥

65. Ādinātha propounded 1¼ crore methods of trance, and they are all extant. Of these, the hearing of the anāhata nāda is the only one, the chief, in my opinion.

मुक्तासने स्थितो योगी मुद्रां संधाय शांभवीम्।
शृणुयाद्दक्षिणे कर्णे नादमंतस्थमेकधीः॥ ६६॥

66. Sitting with Mukta Āsana and with the Śām-bhavī Mudrā, the Yogī should hear the sound inside his right ear, with collected mind.

श्रवणपुटनयनयुगलघ्राणमुखानां निरोधनं कार्यम्।
शुद्धासुषुम्नासरणौ स्फुटममलः श्रूयते नादः॥ ६७॥

67. The ears, the eyes, the nose, and the mouth should be closed and then the clear sound is heard in the passage of the Suṣumnā which has been cleansed of all its impurities.

आरंभश्च घटश्चैव तथा परिचयोऽपि च।
निष्पत्तिः सर्वयोगेषु स्यादवस्थाचतुष्टयम्॥ ६८॥

68. In all the Yogas, there are four states : (1) ārambha or the preliminary, (2) Ghaṭa, or the state of a jar, (3) Paricaya (known), (4) Niṣpatti (con-sumate.)

अथारंभावस्था

ब्रह्मग्रंथेर्भवेद्भेदोत्द्यानंदः शून्यसंभवः।
विचित्रः क्वणको देहेऽनाहतः श्रूयते ध्वनि॥ ६९॥

Ārambha Avasthā

69. When the Brahma granthi(in the heart) is pierced through by Prāṇāyāma, then a sort of happiness is experienced in the vacuum of the heart, and the anāhata sounds, like various tinkling sounds of ornaments, are heard in the body.

दिव्यदेहश्च तेजस्वी दिव्यगंधस्त्वरोगवान्।
संपूर्णहृदयः शून्य आरंभो योगवान् भवेत्॥ ७०॥

70. In the ārambha, a Yogī's body becomes divine, glowing, healthy, and emits a divine smell. The whole of his heart becomes void.

अथ घटावस्था

द्वितीयायां घटीकृत्य वायुर्भवति मध्यगः।
दृढासनो भवेद्योगी ज्ञानी देवसमस्तदा॥ ७१॥

The Ghaṭa Avasthā

71. In the second stage, the airs are united into one and begin moving in the middle channel. The Yogī's posture becomes firm, and he becomes wise like a god.

विष्णुग्रंथेस्ततो भेदात्परमानंदसूचकः।
अतिशून्ये विमर्ददच भेरीशब्दस्तथा भवेत्॥ ७२॥

72. By this means the Viṣṇu knot (in the throat) is pierced which is indicated by highest pleasure experienced, and then the Bherī sound (like the beating of a kettle drum) is evolved in the vacuum in the throat.

अथ परिचयावस्था

तृतीयायां तु विज्ञेयो विहायोमर्दलध्वनिः।
महाशून्यं तदा याति सर्वसिद्धिसमाश्रयम्॥ ७३॥

The Paricaya Avasthā

73. In the third stage, the sound of a drum is known to arise in the Śūnya between the eyebrows, and then the Vāyu goes to the Mahāśūnya, which is the home of all the siddhīs.

चित्तानंदं तदा जित्वा सहजानंदसंभवः।
दोषदुःखजराव्याधिक्षुधानिद्राविवर्जितः॥ ७४॥

74. Conquering, then, the pleasures of the mind, ecstacy is spontaneously produced which is devoid of evils, pains, old age, disease, hunger and sleep.

रुद्रग्रंथिं यदा भित्वा शर्वपीठगतोऽनिलः।
निष्पत्तौ वैणवः शब्दः क्वणद्वीणाक्वणो भवेत्॥ ७५॥

75. When the Rudra granthi is pierced and the air enters the seat of the Lord (the space between the eyebrows), then the perfect sound like that of a flute is produced.

एकीभूतं तदा चित्तं राजयोगाभिधानकम्।
सृष्टिसंहारकर्तासौ योगीश्वरसमो भवेत्॥ ७६॥

76. The union of the mind and the sound is called the Rāja-Yoga, The (real) Yogī becomes the creator and destroyer of the universe, like God.

अस्तु वा मास्तु वा मुक्तिरत्रैवाखंडितं सुखम्।
लयोद्भवमिदं सौख्यं राजयोगादवाप्यते॥ ७७॥

77. Perpetual Happiness is achieved by this; I do not care if the mukti be not attained. This happiness, resulting from absorption [in Brahma], is obtained by means of Rāja-Yoga.

राजयोगमजानंतः केवलं हठकर्मिणाः।
एतानभ्यासिनो मन्ये प्रयासफलवर्जितान्॥ ७८॥

78. Those who are ignorant of the Rāja-Yoga and practise only the Haṭha-Yoga, will, in my opinion, waste their energy fruitlessly.

उन्मन्यवाप्त्ये शीघ्रं भ्रूध्यानं मम संमतम्।
राजयोगपदं प्राप्तं सुखोपायोऽल्पचेतसाम्।
सद्यः प्रत्ययसंधायी जायते नादजो लयः॥ ७९॥

79. Contemplation on the space between the eyebrows is, in my opinion, best for accomplishing soon the *Unmanī* state. For people of small intellect, it is a very easy method for obtaining perfection in the Rāja-Yoga. The Laya produced by nāda, at once gives experience (of spiritual powers).

नादानुसंधानसमाधिभाजां योगीश्वराणां हृदिवर्धमानम्।
आनंदमेकं वचसामगम्यं जानाति तं श्रीगुरुनाथ एक॥ ८०॥

80. The happiness which increases in the hearts of Yogīśvaras, who have gained success in Samādhi by means of attention to the nāda, is beyond des-cription, and is known to *Śri Guru Nātha* alone.

कर्णौ पिधाय हस्ताभ्यां यं शृणोति ध्वनिं मुनिः।
तत्र चित्तं स्थिरीकुर्याद्यावत्स्थिरपदं व्रजेत्॥ ८१॥
(अभ्यस्यमानो नादोऽयं बाह्यमावृणुते ध्वनिं मुनिः।
तत्र चित्तं स्थिरीकुर्याद्यावत्स्थिरपदं व्रजेत्॥ ८१॥)

81. The sound which a muni hears by closing his ears with his fingers, should be heard attentively, till the mind becomes steady in it.

अभ्यास्यमानो नादोऽयं बाह्यमावृणुते ध्वनिम्।
पक्षाद्विक्षेपमाखिलं जित्वा योगी सुखी भवेत्॥ ८२॥

82. By practising with this nāda, all other external sounds are stopped. The Yogī becomes happy by overcoming all distractions within 15 days.

श्रूयते प्रथमाभ्यासे नादो नानाविधो महान्।
ततोऽभ्यासे वर्धमाने श्रूयते सूक्ष्मकः॥ ८३॥

83. In the beginning, the sounds heard are of great

variety and very loud; but, as the practice increases, they become more and more subtle.

आदौ जलधिजीमूतभेरीझर्झरसंभवाः।
मध्ये मर्दलशंखोत्था घंटाकाहलजास्तथा॥ ८४॥

84. In the first stage, the sounds are surging, thundering like the beating of kettle drums and jingling ones. In the intermediate stage, they are like those produced by conch, *Mṛdaṅga,* bells, etc.

अंते तु किंकिणीवंशवीणाभ्रमरनिःस्वनाः।
इति नानाविधा नादाः श्रूयंते देहमध्यगाः॥ ८५॥

85. In the last stage, the sounds resemble those from tinklets, flute, Vīṇā, bee, etc. These various kinds of sounds are heard as being produced in the body.

महति श्रूयमाणेऽपि मेघभेर्यादिके ध्वनौ।
तत्र सूक्ष्मात्सूक्ष्मतरं नादमेव परामृशेत्॥ ८६॥

86. Though hearing loud sounds like those of thunder, kettle drums, etc., one should practise with the subtle sounds also.

घनत्सृज्य वा सूक्ष्मे सूक्ष्ममुत्सृज्य वा घने।
रममाणमपि क्षिप्तं मनो नान्यत्र चालयेत्॥ ८७॥

87. Leaving the loudest, taking up the subtle one, and leaving the subtle one, taking up the loudest, thus practising, the distracted mind does not wander elsewhere.

यत्रकुत्रापि वा नादे लगति प्रथमं मनः।
तत्रैव सुस्थिरीभूय तेन सार्धं विलीयते॥ ८८॥

88. Wherever the mind attaches itself first, it becomes steady there; and then it becomes absorbed in it.

मकरंदं पिबन् भृंगो गंधं नापेक्षते यथा।
नादासक्तं तथा चित्तं विषयान्नहि कांक्षते॥ ८९॥

89. Just as a bee, drinking sweet juice, does not care for the smell of the flower; so the mind, absorbed in the nāda, does not desire the objects of enjoyment.

मनोमत्तगजेंद्रस्य विषयोद्यानचारिणः।
नियमने समर्थोऽयं निनादनिशितांकुशः॥ ९०॥

90. The mind, like an elephant habituated to wander in the garden of enjoyments, is capable of being controlled by the sharp goad of anāhata nāda.

बद्धं तु नादबंधेन मनः संत्यक्तचापलम्।
प्रयाति सुतरां स्थैर्यं छिन्नपक्षः खगो यथा॥ ९१॥

91. The mind, captivated in the snare of nāda, gives up all its activity; and, like a bird with clipped wings, becomes calm at once.

सर्वचिंतां परित्यज्य सावधानेन चेतसा।
नाद एवानुसंधेयो योगसाम्राज्यमिच्छता॥ ९२॥

92. Those desirous of the kingdom of Yoga, should take up the practice of hearing the anāhata nāda, with mind collected and free from all cares.

नादोऽतरंगसारंगबंधने वागुरायते।
अंतरंगकुरंगस्य वधे व्याधायतेऽपि च॥ ९३॥

93. Nāda is the snare for catching the mind; and, when it is caught like a deer, it can be killed also like it.

अंतरंगस्य यमिनो वाजिनः परिघायते।
नादोपास्तिरतो नित्यमवधार्या हि योगिना॥ ९४॥

94. Nāda is the bolt of the stable door for the horse (the minds of the Yogīs). A Yogī should determine to practise constantly in the hearing of the nāda sounds.

बद्धं विमुक्तचांचल्यं नादगंधकजारणात्।
मनः पारदमाप्नोति निरालंबाख्यखेऽटनम्॥ ९५॥

95. Mind gets the properties of calcined mercury. When deprived of its unsteadiness it is calcined, combined with the sulphur of nāda, and then it roams like it in the supportless ākāśa or Brahma.

नादश्रवणतः क्षिप्रमंतरंगभुजंगमः।
विस्मृत्य सर्वमेकाग्रः कुत्रचिन्नहि धावति॥ ९६॥

96. The mind is like a serpent, forgetting all its unsteadiness by hearing the nāda, it does not run away anywhere.

काष्ठे प्रवर्तितो वह्निः काष्ठेन सह शाम्यति।
नादे प्रवर्तितं चित्तं नादेन सह लीयते॥ ९७॥

97. The fire, catching firewood, is extinguished along with it (after burning it up); and so the mind also, working with the nāda, becomes latent along with it.

घंटादिनादसक्तस्तब्धांतःकरणहरिणस्य।
प्रहरणमपि सुकरं शरसंधानप्रवीणश्चेत्॥ ९८॥

98. The antaḥkaraṇa (mind), like a deer, becomes absorbed and motionless on hearing the sound of bells, etc.; and then it is very easy for an expert archer to kill it.

अनाहतस्य शब्दस्य ध्वनिर्य उपलभ्यते।
ध्वनेरंतर्गतं ज्ञेयं ज्ञेयस्यांतर्गतं मनः।
मनस्तत्र लयं याति तद्विष्णोः परमं पदं॥ ९९॥

99. The knowable interpenetrates the anāhata sound which is heard, and the mind interpenetrates the knowable. The mind becomes absorbed there, which is the seat of the all-pervading, almighty Lord.

तावदाकाशसंकल्पो यावच्छब्दः प्रवर्तते।
निःशब्दं तत्परं ब्रह्म परमात्मेति गीयते॥ १००॥

100. So long as the sounds continue, there is the idea of ākāśa. When they disappear, then it is called Para Brahma, Paramātman.

यत्किंचिन्नादरूपेण श्रूयते शक्तिरेव सा।
यस्तत्त्वांतो निराकारः स एव परमेश्वरः॥ १०१॥

101. Whatever is heard in the form of nāda, is the śakti (power). That which is formless, the final state of the Tattvas, is the Parmeśvara.

सर्वे हठलयोपाया राजयोगस्य सिद्धये।
राजयोगसमारूढः पुरुषः कालवंचकः॥ १०२॥

102. All the methods of Haṭha are meant for gaining success in the Rāja-Yoga; for, the man, who is well-established in the Rāja-Yoga, overcomes death.

तत्त्वं बीजं हठः क्षेत्रमौदासीन्यं जलं त्रिभिः।
उन्मनी कल्पलतिका सद्य एव प्रवर्तते॥ १०३॥

103. Tattva is the seed, Haṭha the field; and Indifference (Vairāgya) the water. By the action of these three, the creeper Unmanī thrives very rapidly

सदा नादानुसंधानात् क्षीयंते पापसंचयाः।
निरंजने विलीयेते निश्चितं चित्तमारुतौ॥ १०४॥

104. All the accumulations of sins are destroyed by practising always with the nāda; and the mind and the airs do certainly become latent in the colorless (Paramātman).

शंखदुंदुभिनादं च न शृणोति कदाचन।
काष्ठवज्जायते देह उन्मन्यवस्थायाध्रुवम्॥ १०५॥

105. Such a one does not hear the noise of the conch and Dundubhi. Being in the Unmanī avasthā, his body becomes like a piece of wood.

सर्वावस्थाविनिर्मुक्तः सर्वचिंताविवर्जितः।
मृतवत्तिष्ठते योगी स मुक्तो नात्र संशयः॥ १०६।

106. There is no doubt, such a Yogī becomes free from all states, from all cares, and remains like one dead.

खाद्यते न च कालेन बाध्यते न च कर्मणा।
साध्यते न स केनापि योगी युक्तः समाधिना॥ १०७॥

107. He is not devoured by death, is not bound by his actions. The Yogī who is engaged in Samādhi is overpowered by none.

न गंधं न रसं रूपं न च स्पर्शं न निःस्वनम्।
नात्मानं न परं वेत्ति योगी युक्तः समाधिना॥ १०८॥

108. The Yogī, engaged in Samādhi, feels neither smell, taste, color, touch, sound, nor is conscious of his own self.

चित्तं न सुप्तं नोजाग्रत्स्मृतिविस्मृतिवर्जितम्।
न चास्तमेति नोदेति यस्यासौ मुक्त एव सः।। १०९।।

109. He whose mind is neither sleeping, waking, remembering, destitute of memory, disappearing nor appearing, is liberated.

न विजानाति शीतोष्णं न दुःखं न सुखं तथा।
न मानं नापमानं च योगी युक्तः समाधिना।। ११०।।

110. He feels neither heat, cold, pain, pleasure, respect nor disrespect. Such a Yogī is absorbed in Samādhi.

स्वस्थो जाग्रदवस्थायां सुप्तवद्योऽवतिष्ठते।
निःश्वासोच्छ्वासहीनश्च निश्चितं मुक्त एव सः।। १११।।

111. He who, though awake, appears like one sleeping, and is without inspiration and expiration, is certainly free.

अवध्यः सर्वशस्त्राणामशक्यः सर्वदेहिनाम्।
अग्राह्यो मंत्रयंत्राणां योगी युक्तः समाधिना।। ११२।।

112. The Yogī, engaged in Samādhi, cannot be killed by any instrument, and is beyond the controlling power of beings. He is beyond the reach of incan-tations and charms.

यावन्नैव प्रविशति चरन्मारुतो मध्यमार्गे।
यावद्बिंदुर्न भवति दृढप्राणवातप्रबंधात्।
यावद्ध्याने सहजसदृशं जायते नैव तत्त्वं।
तावज्ज्ञानं वदति तदिदं दंभमिथ्याप्रलापः।। ११३।।

113. As long as the Prāṇa does not enter and flow in the middle channel and the *bindu* does not become firm by the control of the movements of the Prāṇa; as long as the mind does not assume the form of Brahma without any effort in contemplation, so long all the talk of knowledge and wisdom is merely the nonsensical babbling of a mad man.

इति हठप्रदीपिकायां समाधिलक्षणं नाम चतुर्थोपदेशः।। ॐ।।

End of chapter IV, On Samādhi.